GETTING WHAT YOU WANT

GETTING WHAT YOU WANT

The Seven Principles
of Rational Living

ROBERT J. RINGER

G. P. PUTNAM'S SONS
New York

Most Putnam books are available at special quantity discounts for bulk purchases for sales promotions, premiums, fund-raising, and educational needs. Special books or book excerpts also can be created to fit specific needs. For details, write or telephone Putnam Special Markets, 375 Hudson Street, New York, NY 10014.

G. P. Putnam's Sons
a member of
Penguin Putnam Inc.
375 Hudson Street
New York, NY 10014

Library of Congress Cataloging-in-Publication Data

Ringer, Robert J.
    Getting what you want: the seven principles of
      rational living/Robert J. Ringer.   p.   cm.
    ISBN 0-399-14686-5
     1. Conduct of life.   I. Title.
    BJ1581.2.R565   2000   00-028535
    158.1—dc21

Printed in the United States of America

10 9 8 7 6 5 4 3 2 1

This book is printed on acid-free paper. ∞

BOOK DESIGN BY MAUNA EICHNER
INTERIOR ILLUSTRATIONS BY JOHN LARA

Dedicated to those courageous individuals
who dare to think rational thoughts
in an increasingly irrational world

CONTENTS

INTRODUCTION   1

1 **THE WORLD ACCORDING TO YOU**
Principle #1: Base Your Actions on Truth.   5

2 **GET A LIFE**
Principle #2: Focus on Value, Not Entitlements.   37

3 **CHARACTER OF THE SOUL**
Principle #3: Make Choices with Civility, Dignity,
Honesty, and Humility.   71

4 **PEOPLE TAXES**
Principle #4: Avoid Those Who Drain Your
Personal Resources.   101

5 **FREEDOM FROM**
Principle #5: Rid Yourself of Major Encumbrances.   145

6   **TOUGH CHOICES**
*Principle #6: Develop the Self-Discipline to Act
on Intellect Rather Than Impulse.*   189

7   **INJUSTICE FOR ALL**
Principle #7: Learn from Bad Breaks, and Move On.   215

AFTERWORD: THE ENDGAME   245

GETTING WHAT YOU WANT

INTRODUCTION

This book is about getting what you want in life, whether it be friendship, love, money, respect, or just about anything else that you believe will make you happy. There have, of course, been thousands of books written on the subject of achieving happiness, each offering the author's views on how to bring about that much-sought-after, but very elusive, state of mind.

The reason I wrote this book is because I have not found in any other work on the subject what I believe to be the most important key to getting what you want in life. In my view, if the endgame is happiness, and happiness is a result of getting what you want, then the means (or key) to that end is rational living.

Living a rational life is not as easy as it might sound, because the fact is that we are living in an increasingly irrational world—a world where criminals go free on legal technicalities, where we're forced to deal with automated voices instead of human beings when calling large (and sometimes even small) companies, and where sports figures are placed on pedestals high above medical researchers. What I hope to accomplish in this book is to give you specific principles and steps that are foundational to living a rational life, which in turn will allow you to get what you want more easily, more quickly, and with greater confidence.

For the record, I would like to define a rational life as a life guided by the conscious effort to make rational decisions that result in an individual's getting what he wants over the long term, so long as the actions stemming from those decisions do not involve the use of force or fraud against anyone else. In simpler terms, living a rational life begins with the belief that you have a moral right to do what is in your best interest, provided you do not commit aggression against others.

> Rational living requires:
> 1. Conscious effort
> 2. Rational decisions
> 3. Long-term thinking
> 4. An absence of aggression

It goes without saying that someone else's ego being harmed by your happiness or success, or another person's experiencing deep emotional pain as a result of his* uncontrolled envy of you, does not equate to aggression. Such an unfortunate mind set stems from the afflicted person's own neuroses, and by no stretch of the imagination is it your job to spend your waking hours trying to heal sick minds (unless, of course, you're a psychologist, in which case I would suggest you would be a lot more productive if you would have the neurotic individual in question call your receptionist for an appointment).

Long-term thinking is a critical aspect of getting what you want through rational living, because short-term pleasure can be self-destructive if not weighed against long-term consequences. If, for example, a spouse is unfaithful, it may bring him short-

---

*Because I find it cumbersome to use hybrid pronouns such as "his/hers," and am opposed to debasing the English language by mixing singular nouns and pronouns with plural pronouns such as "they," I have, for convenience purposes only, chosen to use the masculine gender throughout this book in most instances where the neuter has not been employed.

term pleasure, but the long-term result could be a lifetime of pain. It is self-evident that thinking only short term is not a rational way to live one's life.

It is also important to understand that getting what you want does not preclude your being kind, charitable, or civic-minded. Nor does it prevent you from being a team player or building meaningful, enduring relationships. All these, and more, can result in a great deal of long-term happiness. It does, however, mean that you have no moral obligation to submit to playing the role of sacrificial lamb whose interests, goals, and happiness are forever subordinated to the interests, goals, and happiness of everyone with whom you come in contact—particularly those whom you do not count among your family, friends, and loved ones. Trying to please everyone is a well-known formula for failure.

Clearly, then, not only does your achieving happiness and success not in any way harm others, it puts you in a position to make constructive contributions to loved ones and, through the invisible hand of the marketplace, the world in general.

I WOULD ALSO like to point out that in this book, as in many of my previous works, you will note a somewhat self-deprecating, hopefully charming character known as "The Tortoise" popping up on a number of pages. The Tortoise entered the world through my first book, *Winning through Intimidation*, where I adopted him as my alter ego, so to speak. I was prompted to do so because many of the anecdotes in that book were reminiscent of the legendary tortoise-and-hare tale.

The Tortoise is the unglamorous plodder who always seems to find a way to come out ahead, though he has a habit of getting bruised and battered along the way. He isn't flashy or impressive; his strengths are consistency, perseverance, and resiliency. He is the classic antihero—Dustin Hoffman as the shy, stuttering boyfriend who ends up with the girl in *The Graduate*, or perhaps former Boston Celtic Larry Bird, the slow, almost awkward, Hall of Famer who always seemed to find a way to win.

The Tortoise's motto is: *If you slow down enough to look over your right shoulder, I'll pass you on the left; if you slow down enough to look over your left shoulder, I'll pass you on the right; and if you try to stop me from passing you on either side, I'll maneuver between your legs if that's what it takes. That heavy breathing you hear behind you is me— steadily closing in on you.*

Or, in more direct terms: Quickly getting out of the starting blocks may get people's attention, but all that counts is where you are when the race is over. The Tortoise is the rational-living poster boy, not only because he focuses on long-term results, but because he's both relentless and resourceful. He's the kind of reptile who, upon being told he can't play in someone's game, simply goes out and starts his own league.

ONE SUGGESTION before we move on: As you read through the following chapters, make a conscious effort to focus on what it is you want in life, and try to link your goal(s) directly to the principles and steps discussed therein. These, I am convinced, are the keys to living a rational life, and it is a rational life that provides the means for achieving virtually any moral goal you may have.

ROBERT J. RINGER

1

THE WORLD ACCORDING TO YOU

Principle #1: Base Your Actions on Truth.

> The truth is incontrovertible.
> Malice may attack it and
> ignorance may deride it,
> but in the end, there it is.
> **WINSTON CHURCHILL**

Human beings have debated the ultimate purpose of life throughout recorded history. If one wanted to participate in this debate, he could make a persuasive argument that the ultimate purpose of life is to search for truth. I say *search* rather than *find*, because to find truth in the broadest sense of the word would mean that one would have to know everything, and I think we can stipulate that omniscience and human beings don't match up too well.

As people have become educated about our court systems through recent high-profile cases, they have discovered, to their considerable dismay, that a legal trial is not a search for truth. I believe that the reason this reality has been such a surprise to most people is because truth is the very foundation not only of the legal systems of the Western world, but of life itself. Truth is the ultimate certitude. Without truth as a foundation, life as we know it could not exist.

Happily, getting what you want in life is not about courtroom justice. It's about you. Therefore, even if the whole world goes insane (a prospect with a reasonably high degree of probability), you have a holy responsibility to yourself to perpetually search for truth. When all about you are losing their heads, the surest way to keep yours is to be vigilant about basing your actions on truth. Conscious life choices are needed to achieve positive results, but that is all but impossible if your premises are false. Truth, then, is the very foundation for getting what you want, and rational thought and actions are the surest way to arrive at truth.

I'm not talking here about *"the* search for truth" or *"a* search for truth." What I'm referring to is *your* search for truth. On the other hand, the words in this chapter—and, indeed, this entire book—represent *my* truth (or, more accurately, my perception of truth). You can accept some, any, or all of my opinions. To whatever degree it is that you concur with what I'm saying, however, I will have accomplished my purpose if *my* truth inspires you to search for *your* truth, because truth is the best friend you will ever have. Unlike people, truth will never desert you in your time of need.

Unfortunately, truth is not an easy proposition. For one thing, truth can sometimes make you unpopular. In extreme cases it has even cost people their lives. Bruno (burned at the stake as a heretic) and Socrates (forced to drink poison after being accused of corrupting youth by questioning tradition) are two well-known examples of this. As a baseline, then, anyone searching for truth must desire truth more than popularity. As we have all witnessed, fools are often among the most popular

> Question everything, even if it represents generations of conventional wisdom.

people in society. This being the case, you must not allow your search for truth to be stifled by the widespread delusions of the masses. Which means you must learn to question everything, even if it represents generations of so-called conventional wisdom.

In the short term, truth can be violated. Rational living, however, calls for making decisions that result in getting what you want over the *long term*. Fortunately, history has repeatedly demonstrated that time is extremely kind to truth.

Given that it's the foundation of getting what you want in life, it is important to carefully dissect truth so there is no doubt about what it entails. Truth, being the vast subject it is, is much more digestible if viewed on three levels.

LEVEL 1: ULTIMATE TRUTH

By Ultimate Truth, I am loosely referring to an understanding of what, if anything, controls the universe. And while an in-depth discussion of Ultimate Truth is beyond the scope of this book, there are some cursory points that need to be addressed, because your pursuit of Ultimate Truth will have an impact on how you pursue other kinds of truths.

Oversimplified, one either believes in the existence of a conscious force governing the universe or he believes the universe is random. In theory, there is actually a third alternative, that being a universe wherein seemingly supernatural events occur, but where no supernatural force is behind them. In the latter case, the universe is seen as pilotless, yet it appears to operate in a precise fashion. An atheist's belief in reincarnation is a good example of this.

Fundamentalism, in the generic sense, is the strict adherence to a set of ideas, and is by definition at odds with a search for truth. This is so whether it be fundamentalist Christianity, fundamentalist Judaism, or fundamentalist atheism. In all cases, fundamentalism closes the door to a serious search for truth.

For example, when someone starts with the premise that the Bible is the word of God, or, in the alternative, starts with the premise that there is no God, his premise is really a personal conclusion. The fact that he feels the need to disguise his own conclusion as a general premise merely demonstrates a lack of belief. God is certainly strong enough to withstand investigation, and, likewise, a rational atheist should feel confident about his ability to back up his anti-God beliefs with facts.

In this regard, one of the best books a fundamentalist religionist can read is George H. Smith's *Atheism: The Case Against God*. It is a brilliant, detailed, relentlessly logical presentation of every conceivable argument against God's existence. If a religionist is willing to analyze with an open mind the kind of powerful information contained in this book, yet still retain his belief in God, it is impressive evidence that his belief is strong.

I would make the same argument for a historical book about Christianity entitled *A History of Christianity*. This work, written by English historian Paul Johnson, is impeccably researched and remarkably detailed, even to the point of discussing factual evidence that places the virgin birth in historical context.

I recall years ago telling a Christian-fundamentalist acquaintance about *A History of Christianity*, which noticeably angered him. He insisted that authors who write books such as this have an atheist agenda, and that he therefore would never read such a book. Interestingly, though, Paul Johnson is not an atheist. He is a practicing Christian who feels that his beliefs are strong enough to stand up to historical truth.

On the other side of the coin, I once suggested to a hardcore atheist friend that there is actually strong mathematical support for the idea that there is a conscious Being at the controls of the universe. As Guy Murchie points out in his remarkable book, *The Seven Mysteries of Life,* an intellectual, long-standing argument for a random universe wherein a seeming miracle such as evolution could take place is that given enough time, anything—including the evolution of human beings from inanimate matter—is possible. This argument, says Murchie, is based on the premise that if you could sit enough billions of chimpanzees in front of computers for enough billions of years, random chance would allow them to write all the great works of literature. Which sounds nice until you consider the mathematics involved.

There are approximately fifty possible letters, numbers, and punctuation marks on a computer keyboard, and there are sixty-five character spaces per line in the average book. Thus, a chimp would have one in fifty chances of getting the first space on the first line correct. Since the same is true of the second space on that line, the chimp would have one chance in 50×50, or 50^2, of getting both spaces right (meaning just the first two letters of the first word of just *one* of the great works of literature). For all sixty-five spaces on the first line, the figure would jump to 50^{65}, which is equal to 10^{110}.

How big is 10^{110}? According to physicist George Gamow, says Murchie, it is a thousand times greater than the total number of vibrations made by all the atoms in the universe since the Big Bang!

Conclusion: It doesn't matter how many chimpanzees or how much time you allow, not even one line of one great work could come into existence through pure chance. As I rhetorically asked my atheist friend, given that you are infinitely more complex than one line of a book, what are the odds that you accidentally, with all your billions of precise, specialized cells, evolved from rocks and dirt over a period of a few billion years?

With noticeable disinterest, he listened to what I had to say, then replied, "To even consider anything that implies there could be a God would destroy the very foundation upon which

I've built my life." I was quite surprised that such an intelligent, rational individual would close his mind to any kind of search that didn't align with his current belief structure.

In the final analysis, the real truth to the Ultimate Truth is that a person who claims to have found it cannot prove it to anyone else. He must be satisfied with contentment within himself. Likewise, no one can disprove another person's claim that he has discovered Ultimate Truth. The search for Ultimate Truth is very personal in nature and, consciously or otherwise, is the foundation—the starting point, if you will—for how each individual goes about living his life.

LEVEL 2: SCIENTIFIC TRUTH

Science is based on universal principles, or laws. You cannot create or alter a principle. A principle is a natural law that has always existed and will continue to exist as long as there is a universe. We cannot change principles or create new ones; we can only try to discover them, then find ways to use them to our advantage.

Gravity is the most commonly used example of a scientific principle. We know that anything that falls within the earth's atmosphere will accelerate toward the ground at the rate of 32 ft/sec^2. There are no exceptions to this law. The same is true of molecular structure. Identical atoms under the same pressure at the same temperature will always combine to form the same molecules. Or Newton's Third Law of Motion, which states that for every action there is an equal and opposite reaction. It would be accurate to say that the umbrella principle for all scientific principles is: *Actions have consequences that are always in accordance with the laws of science.*

A scientific principle is truth in its purist form. When we discover scientific truths and use our creativity to apply these truths in positive ways, we accomplish positive results. Nowadays, most of us don't even give a second thought to these results, whether it be flying to the moon, dramatically increasing food production, or producing everything from CD players to jumbo jets. As our understanding of scientific principles continues to accelerate, yesterday's luxuries are increasingly viewed by the average person as necessities.

Many people believe that scientific truth collides with Ultimate Truth—i.e., that it invalidates God—in that God becomes irrelevant in the face of scientific explanations of the nature of the Universe. But does He? There is near unanimity among scientists regarding the occurrence of the so-called "Big Bang" about 14 billion years ago, as well as the belief that the first atoms formed were hydrogen gas. However, what is still baffling to scientists is how the stars, galaxies, clusters of galaxies, and superclusters formed out of uniformly smooth hydrogen gas.

Even more baffling is the recent discovery that the formation of the substantive universe is not at all random; rather, the galaxies form precise patterns. I recently watched a documentary about space in which the narrator at one point asked, "What unknown forces in the early universe could have created these vast structures?" Call it God, call it a Supernatural Force, call it the Cosmic Mind, call it Mysteries of Life if that's what it takes to quell humanist fears of a Controlling Force, but there certainly is compelling evidence that the universe may, in fact, not be random.

Increasingly, a growing number of astronomers and space physicists seem to be expressing doubts about a random universe. What is finally being addressed is the fact that science can explain, say, *how* gravity works, but it cannot explain *why* it works the way it does. In other words, gravity explains what makes the planets, stars, galaxies, and other heavenly bodies act on each other the way they do, but it does nothing to explain how the principle of gravity came into being.

Robert Jastrow, founder of NASA's Goddard Institute for Space Studies, in his book, *God and the Astronomers,* tied scientific truth to Ultimate Truth in an interesting way when he said:

"For the scientist who has lived by his faith in the power of reason, the story ends like a bad dream. He has scaled the mountains of ignorance; he is about to conquer the highest peak; as he pulls himself over the final rock, he is greeted by a band of theologians who have been sitting there for centuries." Thus, the chasm between theologians and scientists seems to be narrowing toward a middle-ground belief that science is not in conflict with God, but, rather, is a gift of God.

While it is unlikely that any of us will ever have proof that there is a connection between scientific truth and Ultimate Truth, with regard to our daily lives it is important for us to understand that any attempt to act in violation of scientific truth results in bad consequences. It matters not whether the violation is intentional or a result of ignorance; in either case, scientific truth yields the same consequences. The cigarettes that kill you have little interest in whether or not you were aware of their lethal nature.

LEVEL 3: SECULAR TRUTH

By *secular truth*, I am referring to "the way the world works." Ultimate Truth is very personal in nature, and scientific truth is not something most of us have to consciously think about in our daily lives. But each of us has to deal with secular truth every day. We therefore have to have a reasonably good batting average when it comes to deciphering secular truth.

As with scientific law, the umbrella principle here—albeit more general in nature—is that *actions have consequences*. Children and politicians are notorious for either not understanding the consequences of their actions or refusing to believe that the same action will always result in the same consequence. (It is fascinating to ponder why we punish children for not heeding the consequences of their actions, yet vote for politicians who promise to ignore history and continue to repeat the same mistakes.)

Like scientific truth, secular truth brings the same results regardless of our intentions. Secular truth cares nothing about whether we think it is just or unjust; our feelings are irrelevant. Most people understand this reality on an intellectual level, but continually reject it on an emotional level, as demonstrated by the way they live their lives. Why else would people drive while intoxicated? Or lie in an effort to get out of a tight spot? Or live beyond their means? Or commit crimes?

What makes secular truth such a tricky proposition is that our observations are made through the eyes of our individual conditioning. Thus, your truth may be very different from my truth because of our personal experiences. One person may see the flag of his country as a symbol of freedom; another person may see it as a symbol of oppression. The difference lies in their belief structures.

This is what happened in the infamous O. J. Simpson trial. Most people, including a significant percentage of African-Americans, were appalled at how (primarily) black jurors could allow a vicious murderer to walk free. It wasn't that those jurors believed murder was okay. It was that their negative experiences with police blinded them to the point where they were able to ignore the overwhelming evidence and allow a band of truth-twisting attorneys to switch their focus to unrelated topics such as racism and police corruption. As hundreds of millions of people around the world witnessed with amazement, Simpson's hired legal guns were so good at their craft that they ultimately succeeded in transforming the proceedings into the trial of Mark Fuhrman and the Los Angeles Police Department.

What causes perceptions, and therefore conclusions, to be wrong are flawed conditioning, false premises, and false assumptions. Unfortunately, probably a majority of false premises are learned as a small child and carried through life. Which leads to the obvious question, how can a person's life possibly turn out well if a significant percentage of his perceptions and actions are based on incorrect premises? Since an incorrect premise or assumption is a falsehood, there is a snowballing effect; i.e., an untrue premise or assumption leads to an untrue perception, which in turn leads to other untrue premises, assumptions, and perceptions. All of which lead to action contrary to one's best interest, which in turn results in pain.

By contrast, the path to pleasure is paved with correct premises and assumptions, which in turn lead to correct perceptions. And basing your actions on correct perceptions makes it infinitely more likely that you will get what you want in life.

> The path to pleasure is paved with correct premises and assumptions, which in turn lead to correct perceptions.

IN THIS REGARD, I am reminded of a story I first heard from a longtime friend, John Pugsley. Imagine you are adrift at sea. You wash up on an island, where you are taken in by a tribe of friendly, intelligent natives. You are initially thankful for your good fortune. However, you discover that all is not well in the village. For generations the villagers have been engaged in a bloody, ongoing war with another tribe on the opposite side of the island. They are in a high state of anxiety over an upcoming battle, a battle which if they win will destroy their enemy and end the tortuous war, but if they lose could lead to their own destruction and/or enslavement. If they lose, you, too, will be a victim.

There is a divisive argument in progress over the strategy to be employed to win the battle. It is an argument that has raged for generations, and frequently leads to bloodshed within the tribe. The natives are in agreement with the premise that victory is possible only by appeasing the god of the volcano, but they are in dispute over how he is to be appeased.

The elder faction believes the battle can be won only if the god is appeased through the ritual murder of five of the other tribe's most beautiful maidens. The sacrifice must be carried out according to rules set down hundreds of years ago by the tribe's founders. The maidens must be captured in a raid, their heads shaved, blindfolded with palm leaves, bound with vines, and thrown live into a boiling lake in the center of the volcano.

A second group of young radicals is convinced that the ritual has been misinterpreted. To win the battle, this group believes there should be seven maidens, not five, that they should not be shaved, and that they should be killed with a knife.

Both groups are adamant. Both are passionate. The tribe is rigidly and irreconcilably divided. In fact, subfactions are springing up that argue over the details of each plan, but all agree with the premise that ritual kidnapping and sacrifice is essential for victory; they disagree only on the details.

It immediately becomes obvious to you that the capturing and killing of the other tribe's maidens is not the solution to the tribe's problems, but, rather, the very kind of act that has caused the perpetual war.

You enter a hut and find members of the two factions studying ancient drawings of the ritual. They are arguing about a detail. The elders are uncertain only about whether the drawing means the blindfolds should be made of palm leaves or hemp. The younger faction says that it clearly means a knife must be used. They both turn to you and insist that you cast the deciding vote. Which is the correct solution? How do *you* think the maidens should be killed?

What do you say to them? Obviously, you don't think the maidens should be killed at all, but how can you possibly make them see the gross error they are making in their search for a solution to the war? It is easy for us to see that the premise— killing the maidens—is false, but the natives on this island have been conditioned from childhood to accept this hideous premise.

While this may sound like nothing more than a bad dream, in truth you have been cast ashore on just such an island, an island wherein the natives are your fellow citizens and political leaders. On a global scale, nearly 6 billion people are continuously engaged in acrimonious and bitter debate about how to solve an infinite number of problems, most of which are based on false premises.

Your search for truth, then, will be flawed to the same extent as your conditioning and premises are flawed, meaning that you cannot expect to have truth on your terms. To lay down conditions in advance of searching for truth is the height of frivolity. If you want enlightenment on your terms, you will find only illusion and falsehood.

Thus, a prerequisite to searching for truth as a way of getting what you want in life is your willingness to let go of cherished beliefs. The one belief that *is* important to maintain is that neither tradition nor conventional wisdom makes something right. You must be willing to question everything. In the words of Buddha, "Believe nothing, no matter where you read it, or who said it, no matter if I have said it, unless it agrees with your own reason and your own common sense."

A CASE IN POINT is evolution. Like many people, I am fascinated by the subject. Unlike many people, however, I have no ax to grind in this area, because I don't see evolution as necessarily a religious issue. As it has been the focal point of so much debate between religionists on the one hand and atheists and scientists (who may or may not be atheists) on the other, it is a subject that cries out for a serious search for truth.

Interestingly, it has not been that long ago that it was heresy in our schools to teach children about evolution as explained in Charles Darwin's theory of natural selection. The landmark trial of school teacher John Thomas Scopes, argued by William Jennings Bryan and Clarence Darrow, is a case that mesmerized America in 1925. Scopes was found guilty of violating Tennessee law by teaching Darwin's theory to his students, but his case was later overturned by the state supreme court.

Now, however, the evolution of the school system itself has reversed the nature of the problem. Evolution, which is but a theory, is now considered fact by a vast majority of educators. In other words, they state their conclusion as a premise, which, at best, is irrational; at worst, it is deceitful. A child who questions the validity of evolution as it is now taught in virtually all schools is likely to fall into disfavor with his teacher and be heckled by his classmates. Very few teachers have an inclination to debate the subject.

My own fascination with evolution began in high school. I had long before accepted evolution as a fact, and during this period of my life I became highly motivated to read as much as possible about the subject. To my surprise, however, the more I read, the more evolution began to sound like a fairy tale. Inanimate matter "evolving" into an animal, and an animal eventually becoming a human being? Hmmm.

Much as I was predisposed to believing in the validity of the theory of evolution, what I found was that virtually every book on the subject began with the premise that evolution was a fact. In other words, the theory of evolution has been given a dispensation from the requirement to present evidence. For example, not a single fossil has ever been found that demonstrates an intermediary stage between any two supposedly connected species, the so-called missing link for which generations of dedicated paleontologists have been searching.

The coup de grâce, however, was when I read a book entitled *Ever Since Darwin*, written by Stephen Jay Gould, one of the world's leading paleontologists and evolutionary biologists. Like virtually all other authors on the subject, in *Ever Since Darwin* Gould discusses evolution in an *a priori* fashion—i.e., stated as a fact—yet, when he reaches the last page of the book, he states:

"I hope that . . . Darwin's own work will permeate more areas of evolutionary thought, where rigid dogmas still reign as a consequence of unquestioned preference, old habits, or social prejudice. My own favorite target is the belief in slow and steady evolutionary change preached by most paleontologists. . . . *The fossil record does not support it; mass extinction and abrupt origin reign* (my italics)."

Gould, the hard-core evolutionist, is obviously a serious seeker of truth. His truthfulness in admitting that all known evidence suggests that most, if not all, species have appeared on earth suddenly is certainly admirable, though I am in no way suggesting that he believes a Higher Being instantly created either life or any particular species.

Some years after Gould's book was published, a team of French scientists, including representatives from the prestigious Centre des Faibles Radio-activités, concluded that Neanderthal man did not, as had long been assumed, disappear prior to the onset of modern man. Recent evidence suggests that Neanderthal did not become extinct until about 36,000 years ago, which would mean that others of the genus homo coexisted with him and therefore could not have, as many scientists believe, evolved from him. This supports the long-accepted findings that Cro-Magnon man, the prototype of modern man whose skeletal remains were first found in a cave in Southern France, mysteriously and quickly appeared on earth at about the same time as Neanderthal disappeared.

It is, of course, entirely possible that evolution as taught in our schools is correct. But even if evolution were ultimately proven beyond a reasonable doubt, there is still the problem of the billions of chimpanzees pecking away at computer keyboards for billions of years; i.e., evolution in a random universe would appear to be a mathematical impossibility.

Thus, a religionist would have no reason to fear evidence that supports evolution, for it is quite possible that evolution, if there really is such a thing, is not powered by randomness. A Conscious Force may have created evolution, and that Force could still be at the controls. Or, of course, evolution also could be entirely wrong (at least as it relates to one species evolving into another). It could be that a Higher Being created both animals and man in pretty much their present forms.

Whichever it may be, starting with evolution as a premise simply because we have been conditioned to believe it is a fact, or starting with the premise that evolution contradicts the Bible and is therefore off-limits to discuss, only gets in the way of a serious search for truth. It cannot be repeated too often: A prerequisite to searching for truth is one's willingness to let go of cherished beliefs. Those who refuse to give up beliefs that are contrary to the facts are the very people who make it possible for maiden-killing premises to survive.

The Art of Truth Twisting

False premises are one thing, outright lies quite another. The search for truth as a key element in getting what you want is made infinitely more difficult by the fact that we are surrounded by people who spend their lives trying to twist the truth to their own ends. Politicians and leaders of causes (discussed in more detail in Chapter 5) are notoriously prolific truth twisters.

Obviously, no politician today would admit that he obfuscates the truth for the purpose of achieving his own ends, which only makes the daily deluge of lies we receive from our anointed leaders all the more dangerous. These lies condition our minds and lead us to false premises. These premises are cemented in place by those who control the education system, because they have the luxury of rewriting history, an art form that has come to be known as "revisionist history." To the extent that we allow truth twisters to impact our thinking, we are less likely to get what *we* want and more likely to give them what *they* want.

Brainwashing

The spine-chilling message in the movie *The Manchurian Candidate* is that evil-intentioned human beings can capture the thinking mechanisms of other human beings and direct them to take actions that violate their personal moral codes.

The catchphrase used to describe this phenomenon is "brainwashing." Depending upon how broadly one wishes to interpret the phenomenon of brainwashing, it can include anything from mind-dulling ads on television to cult leaders who direct their followers to commit suicide. Beer commercials, for example, seem to want us to believe that if men will just drink more beer, they can spend the remainder of their lives playing volleyball, frolicking on the beach surrounded by beautiful, bikini-clad women, and, above all, laughing hysterically.

Whereas television commercials are relatively harmless, encouraging only the most vulnerable among us to be lazy, ignorant, and short-sighted, cult brainwashing can be quite harmful. Until I moved to New Zealand, I had never given much thought to cults other than to view an occasional Jonestown-type horror story on television. Shortly after my arrival, I developed a friendship with "Jeremy," a highly intelligent, creative entrepreneur with a remarkable work ethic. He was a persuasive, seemingly rational individual with an infectious positive attitude.

I found Jeremy's insights into ideology, human relations, and health matters to be inspiring. I was convinced that he had all the tools necessary not only to be successful in his own right, but to make a positive impact on Kiwi society.

At some point in time, I became aware that Jeremy attended regular weekly meetings of what he described as a "self-help group." He once said to me in passing, "I'm going to press you real hard to become involved in my group," but at the time I didn't give the comment much thought.

A short while later, during one of our discussions about nutrition, Jeremy told me that his group owned an organic farm,

"We work for free, because we believe in self-responsibility."

which he invited me to visit. I accepted his proposal, and a couple of days later we made the trek a few miles out of town to the farm. At the edge of the farm was a sort of open-air shack from which group members sold home-made soup, drinks, and produce grown on-site.

Jeremy introduced me to two young women who were dispensing the hot soup, and invited me to have a bowl. Anatomically speaking, each of us has a microscopic alarm in our brain—referred to in higher circles of medicine as the Kosher Button—that activates when something we're hearing or seeing doesn't ring true. When I heard the two soup-serving women speak, I thought I was talking to the Stepford wives. Whereupon my alarm quickly announced: *Not kosher!* I then looked carefully into their eyes, and the message came back even stronger: *Definitely not kosher!*

When Jeremy and I were walking back to our car, an elderly woman in tattered clothes said hello to him. He introduced her, then later told me that she was a longtime member of the group. It struck me that this woman did not appear to be the kind of person who would be involved in a self-help group to which I imagined Jeremy belonged.

In the coming weeks, I began asking various acquaintances about the group, the farm, the people whom I had met, and Jeremy, and was stunned by the feedback I received. The self-help group, it turned out, was "Money's Gate," an infamous cult that was well known throughout most of New Zealand. Some members had belonged to Money's Gate for more than twenty years. I was told that Jeremy was the number-two man in the cult, just a heartbeat away from ascending the throne.

The man at the top, the cult's leader, was said to be a uniquely wise person who preached self-responsibility. Members were taught that no excuse was justifiable when it came to not meeting one's commitments, which sounded like an admirable foundation for a self-help group.

Unfortunately, many of the group's rules and practices contradicted its purported purpose. For one thing, every member was required to pay the leader of Money's Gate a fixed percentage of his gross weekly income. The money, I was told, was paid in twenty-dollar bills, and slipped under the cult leader's back door in an unmarked envelope or rolled up and pushed through a round hole in the same door. If the leader proclaimed the money count to be incorrect, the member did not receive credit for any of his contribution.

A business acquaintance told me that both of his younger brothers had been recruited into Money's Gate while still in high school. It happened a short time after their father died, which seemed to be a common thread in the recruitment of a number of members. (Jeremy himself had joined the cult in high school, a number of years after his own father had passed away.) After a ten-year tenure, one of the brothers dropped out of the cult, whereupon the other brother was forbidden by members to speak to him.

I also was told by several ex-members that Money's Gate had periodic feasts at which members would sit around a large table, with the seating based on their status in the cult's hierarchy, and pass around sumptuous platters of food. The cult's leader would make his selections first, then pass each platter on to Jeremy. Jeremy would take what he wanted and pass the food on to the next person in the pecking order, and so on until whatever food was left eventually found its way to the lowest member on the cult ladder.

The numerous stories that were related to me about Money's Gate could fill a book of their own, but what was perhaps most surprising was the number of people in the cult who had legitimate occupational backgrounds. Included among its members were graphic artists, cabinet makers, accountants, and various business owners and entrepreneurs. Jeremy himself was an incredibly energetic, bright, hardworking entrepreneur who preached self-responsibility and individualism, and, in addition, appeared to be both logical and rational. All of these positive qualities notwithstanding, I ultimately became convinced that the brainwashing had gone on far too long and that Jeremy was a "lifer."

This eye-opening experience made me realize that neither high intelligence nor rational action in other areas of a person's life will necessarily deter him from buying into a cult's program, no matter how irrational or contradictory that program may be. In other words, quality brainwashing has the power to triumph over quality intellect, sort of like the old baseball maxim that good pitching beats good hitting every time. This is precisely why you are surrounded by millions of intelligent people who are constantly debating how the maidens should be killed. Through the magic of gradualism, governments have succeeded in brainwashing people worldwide into accepting a wide range of false premises.

Rational living and brainwashing clearly are at opposite ends of the self-determination spectrum. Happiness demands, first and foremost, that a person be in control of his mind. To the extent someone else does your thinking for you—be it television commentators, government officials, or leaders of causes—you are likely to make decisions that are not in your best interest. More often than not, such decisions will be based on someone else's view of right and wrong, a view often camouflaged by lies.

In this regard, it is wise to heed the words of Ralph Waldo Emerson, who said, "Nothing is at last sacred but the integrity of your own mind." Anything sacred should be guarded with a passion, which is why you should never allow anyone to gain control of your greatest asset. And the best way to accomplish that is to be vigilant when it comes to relying on your own ability to think rationally as opposed to blindly accepting the opinions of others.

Loving Truth

To effectively use the search for truth as a means to happiness, you must first come to love truth. Clearly, most people do not love truth; instead, they try to make true that which they love. This is what causes people to embrace government handouts; they love the concept of something for nothing. In other words, you have to be careful not to confuse truth with personal desires; i.e., you must be willing to subordinate personal desires to reality.

The failure to love truth is why human beings have such a propensity for shooting messengers. Messengers are the bad guys who have an annoying habit of delivering truth. But no matter how many dead messengers we leave lying at our feet, no matter how vigorously we hide from truth, it always finds a way to survive and deliver its consequences to us. And the consequences can be severe; the greater the repression of truth, and the longer the period of time over which the repression takes place, the graver the ultimate consequences.

Why, then, do people hate truth so much? Because truth can often be harsh, and, as human beings, we quite naturally gravitate toward less pain and more pleasure. But isn't that what rational living is all about? Yes, but only as it pertains to *long-term* results, not instant gratification. We simply do not like our little delusive worlds to be upset by truth. We don't worry about what's coming down the road; we just want to feel good today. But the reality is that one has to be willing to experience the discomfort often associated with truth if his objective is to achieve positive, long-term consequences.

THE SHOOTING OF A MEDICAL MESSENGER

The worldwide medical establishment has long been known for its vigilance in defending the status quo against maverick truth messengers. One of the earliest "heretics" to feel the sting of the American Medical Association's attacks was Dr. Max Gerson, a German immigrant born October 18, 1881, in Wongrowitz, Germany (which later became part of Poland). He attended the universities of Breslau, Würzburg, Berlin, and Freiburg, from 1901 to 1906, then served as an intern at a number of hospitals and clinics throughout Germany.

In 1910, Dr. Gerson, who had suffered from severe migraine headaches for years, came across a book written by an Italian doctor who claimed that some migraine headaches could be relieved by a milk diet, while others could be relieved by a fresh-fruit-and-vegetable diet. He first tried the milk diet, but without success. He then put himself on the fruit-and-vegetable diet, with an emphasis on apples, both raw and cooked. In a short period of time, his migraines disappeared. He then experimented by adding salt and a variety of other substances to the fruits and vegetables, only to find that his migraines returned very quickly, sometimes within a half hour.

After serving in World War I, Dr. Gerson set up practice in Bielefeld, Germany, as an internist and specialist in nervous diseases. Expanding his experimentation with diet, Gerson was successful in curing 446 out of 450 supposedly incurable cases of lupus (an autoimmune disorder characterized by skin lesions). For his work in this area, Dr. Gerson was hopeful that he might earn the Nobel Prize for medicine. To his disbelief, he instead was challenged by the German medical establishment and hauled into court. The charge was that he was not a specialist in skin disorders, and therefore his work in this area was in violation of the German medical code.

After having similar success with "incurable" lung tuberculosis, he again was challenged by the establishment medical community. Unfortunately, before he was able to prove that his natural diet therapy did, in fact, cure lung tuberculosis, Dr. Gerson, who was Jewish, had to flee his homeland because of the increasingly dangerous political situation at that time. After his escape from Germany, Dr. Gerson lived in Vienna, then moved to Ville d'Avray near Paris to become chief of staff of a sanatorium. Finally, after a short stay in England, Dr. Gerson emigrated to the United States.

In New York, at age fifty-five, Dr. Gerson had to go to school with first and second graders to learn how to speak English, a prerequisite for his earning a medical license, which he received in January, 1936, after passing the New York State Board examination. After setting up practice in New York City, Dr. Gerson continued his diet experiments with incurable arthritis and cancer patients. His success rate was astonishing even to him, and it made the medical establishment very uneasy.

On July 3, 1946, Dr. Gerson demonstrated his healing techniques before a U.S. Senate subcommittee headed by Senator Claude Pepper, bringing with him five cancer patients he had cured with his organic fruit-and-vegetable therapy. To put it mildly, the American Medical Association went berserk. In its November 16, 1946, edition, the *Journal of the American Medical Asso-*

ciation stated, "Fortunately for the American people, this presentation received little, if any, newspaper publicity." Later, in its January 8, 1949, edition, the same AMA publication declared, "There is no scientific evidence whatsoever to indicate that modifications in the dietary intake of food or other nutritional essentials are of any specific value in the control of cancer."

The AMA pressured hospitals, laboratories, and other doctors not to do business with Dr. Gerson. This made it difficult for him to document his work, because he was prevented from bringing his patients to established facilities for testing.

The final blow, however, was when Dr. Gerson was invited to be a guest on a radio talk show hosted by the popular Long John Nebel. The show lasted for several hours, and the public's response was overwhelming. The result? The radio network was threatened by the AMA, and Nebel was fired the day after Gerson's appearance.

Finally, on March 8, 1959, after years of harassment from the AMA and other segments of the establishment medical community, Dr. Max Gerson, the ultimate medical messenger, died of pneumonia. In reflecting on Dr. Gerson's work, Albert Schweitzer, the renowned doctor, writer, and musician who won the Nobel Peace Prize in 1952, and whose wife Gerson had cured of lung tuberculosis, said, "I see in him one of the most eminent medical geniuses in the history of medicine . . . Unfortunately, he could not engage in scientific research or teach; and he was greatly impeded by adverse political conditions.

"In ordinary times he would have been able to expound his ideas for many years as professor at one of the important German universities; would have taught pupils who could carry on his research and teachings; would have found recognition and encouragement . . . All this was denied him. His was the hard lot of searching and working as an uprooted immigrant, to be challenged and stand as a fighter. We who knew and understood him admired him for working his way out of discouragement again and again, and for undertaking to conquer the obstacles . . ."

Long after the silencing of Dr. Gerson, corporate giants in the dairy, beef, tobacco, and pharmaceutical industries, along with the American Medical Association, continued to shoot down one medical messenger after another in an effort to repress the hated, profit-killing truth. Growing up, I can remember being encouraged from all quarters (including my parents) to eat plenty of eggs, butter, cheese, milk, white bread, and, above all, good old-fashioned beef. I can even vividly recall Perry Como taking a relaxing puff on his Lucky Strike cigarette, exhaling the fumes, then telling millions of television viewers that Luckies not only tasted good, but were "good for you."

Today, of course, all this sounds like insanity, because just about everyone both in and outside of the medical community fully understands that these are the very things that provide the shortest route to heart disease, stroke, and a wide variety of cancers.

Dr. Gerson was the most hated kind of messenger, because the message he delivered threatened not only the incomes of doctors, but of hospitals, clinics, and those involved in the manufacture and sale of pharmaceuticals and surgical equipment as well. After all, if people ate healthy food, where would the medical community get its patients? Fortunately, today the importance of a natural diet for the prevention, and even cure, of most diseases is pretty well accepted, thanks to professionals like Dr. Andrew Weil who have the luxury of being able to stand on the shoulders of giants like Dr. Gerson. Even though there are those in the medical-pharmaceutical complex who stubbornly continue to take pot shots at the messengers of so-called natural health, there are now so many medical messengers that shooting them is no longer a practical solution.

Happily, dead messengers notwithstanding, history once again has been kind to truth.

Messengers aside, many people live in a world of delusions that blind them from truth. In the case of Dr. Gerson, the medical establishment, for monetary reasons, intentionally blocked the truth from the general public. But many of the falsehoods we harbor are the result of self-inflicted misinformation; i.e., even though we know, or at least suspect, that the facts are contrary to our desires, we choose to ignore these facts and cling to our cherished beliefs. In psychology, the term used to describe the anxiety resulting from this self-destructive state of mind is *cognitive dissonance*. A person so afflicted simply blocks out information that contradicts his established belief structure.

In the case of my friend Jeremy, even though he had obviously experienced years of cult brainwashing, I was convinced from our discussions that the only way he had managed to continue his self-destructive way of life was through intense self-delusion. On the one hand, he preached self-responsibility and individualism, but at the same time he paid homage and money to the leader of Money's Gate because he believed in the cult's hierarchical structure. Clearly, his mind simultaneously held two contradictory beliefs. His anxiety and stress over this conflict were outwardly obvious to those closest to him.

Unless it involves torture-style brainwashing and seclusion, such as that depicted in *The Manchurian Candidate*, I am convinced that at some point in time a brainwashed person must engage in self-delusion in order to continue shielding himself from the truth.

MOST SELF-DELUSION, however, does not involve brainwashing, and where money matters are concerned, this is especially true. It's usually just a case of substituting one's desires for reality. The stock market is a classic example of this. In theory, investing in operating enterprises is a noble activity, because it provides cap-

"Tell us, Mr. Tortoise, where did you acquire your uncanny expertise in stock-market analysis?"

ital and liquidity to the capital markets. But in real life, most people invest in stocks because they believe they can increase their wealth without labor. This is especially true during long bull markets, when the average investor becomes convinced that stock values will continue to rise indefinitely. As every stock-market professional knows, this is pure fantasy.

History notwithstanding, every generation insists on pushing the markets beyond their breaking points, and usually those who can least afford it end up holding the badly deflated bag. Again, self-delusion is the culprit. Given that even the most unsophisticated stock-market players can and do read, they certainly must know that every bull market eventually gives way to a bear market—often a nasty bear market. In addition, at one time or another most investors have read about one of the many studies that have repeatedly demonstrated that throwing darts at a dartboard containing the names of listed stocks often produces better results than does the careful study of many of the most highly touted stock-market experts.

ONE OF THE MOST fascinating forms of self-delusion is the need of so many people to idolize celebrities, building them up in their own minds to be something much more than they are. Celebrity idolatry seems to be a method for artificially acquiring strength when one views his own accomplishments as menial, thus it could be postulated that this kind of self-delusion flows from a lack of self-esteem.

Hard as it is to understand, the cradle of the civilized world, Great Britain, still has a queen. The English love their monarchy, which for many years has provided a windfall for the tabloids. Royalty is one thing, but how about common folk who are placed on pedestals by millions of adoring fans—athletes incapable of uttering an intelligible sentence, movie stars who babble about social justice from behind the walls of their $10 million estates, and recording artists who glorify drugs, sex, and violence in their songs?

Perhaps the greatest myth created by a mysterious and contagious strain of the self-delusion virus is that of Elvis Presley. From afar, Elvis seemed like a nice chap with an interesting face and a good enough voice to allow him to make an excellent living. But that was pretty much it. He never wrote a song, couldn't play a musical instrument (other than barely being able to pluck around on his guitar prop), couldn't act, and put himself into an early grave with a remarkable lack of self-discipline that ballooned his weight and saturated his body with harmful substances. To his credit, he never championed a cause; in fact, he never claimed to believe in anything.

These are the qualifications that get you on a postage stamp? As they say, it's a great country. So how do people manage to delude themselves into believing that so many movie stars, recording artists, and athletes are something they are not? I believe it's a result of man's desperate need to have someone to look up to. We all want the security of knowing that royalty is smiling down on us. After all, we did christen Elvis "The King," and I suspect there's a good bit of Freudian psychology in that.

PERHAPS THE MOST dangerous self-delusion of all is our belief in our own immortality. Of course, we don't admit it, at least not to others. But in our minds, some of us truly believe that we will be the first people to live forever. Why else would a person smoke, take drugs, drink excessively, or eat a diet loaded with fat, sugar, and processed foods?

For more than thirty years, my eldest sister became angry with anyone in the family who tried to encourage her to stop smoking. She said simply that she enjoyed it, notwithstanding the fact that she was a highly intelligent, well-informed person who certainly was aware of the much-publicized facts regarding cigarette smoke.

Sadly, the day the doctor handed my sister her death warrant, a diagnosis of inoperable lung cancer, she immediately stopped smoking. She spent the rest of her days angry with herself for "being so stupid." And, of course, she didn't miss the enjoyment she once got from cigarettes. If you've ever witnessed someone close to you dying of cancer, you know it's a pretty grim scene, one that you never forget. It certainly makes you think long and hard about your own mortality.

In my view, the delusion that allows a person to engage in a dangerous activity with impunity, be it smoking or drunk driving, is based on a hypnotic self-delusion, the belief that he can defy the odds and escape the inevitable consequences of his actions. Coming to grips with one's own mortality is nothing more than a matter of overriding one's wishes with reality.

If truth is the foundation of living a rational life, then the first and most important truth to accept is the reality that you are not immortal. One's own mortality is another one of those truths that most people accept on an intellectual level, but do not really believe on a day-to-day, emotional level. You must therefore be vigilant when it comes to ridding yourself of any self-delusion you may be harboring about your own mortality, then live life accordingly. Ironically, the more you act on the belief that you're immortal, the sooner you are likely to find out, to your dismay, that you are not. A better idea is to live in accordance with truth and enjoy good health while you're here.

The reason you have to be vigilant about this matter is because you will always be surrounded by temptations to eat, drink, and partake in activities that are anti-life. A wise philosopher friend of mine once asked me who the biggest mass murderer in history was. I knew it was a trick question, one to which most people give the knee-jerk response, "Hitler." The correct answer, I felt certain, was Joseph Stalin, the brutal Soviet dictator who killed some 20 million of his own countrymen.

"Wrong," said my friend. "The greatest mass murderer in history was Ray Kroc, founder of McDonald's." I got the message. Ruthless dictators use violence. There is no pretense of fun, no clown frolicking on television in an attempt to convince people that happiness awaits them in the gulag.

The fast-food folks, on the other hand, while publicly supporting charitable causes aimed at saving the planet and helping the poor, maintain fun-looking killing machines throughout the world—colorful little shacks filled with food weapons that turn people's bodies into medical time bombs. Prostate and colon cancer, arteriosclerosis, stroke, and diabetes, while not as spectacular as decapitations and firing squads, succeed year after year in piling up the kind of impressive fatality numbers that would make run-of-the-mill serial killers envious.

P.S.—Don't blame the fast-food executioners if you get killed by a deadly burger, taco, or innocent-looking piece of pizza. These guys are humble. They know full well that they couldn't do it without the help of your self-delusion. Trust me on this one: You *are* mortal. Accept this truth, treat your body with respect, and you may just stick around long enough to enjoy a life worth living.

TRUTH IS WHAT IT IS; people's perception of truth is a variable. However, when another person's perception of truth is inaccurate, that person's inaccurate perception becomes a reality in itself, a reality you have to take into consideration when dealing with him. Put another way, though you may be certain that the other person's belief is untrue, his erroneous *belief*—not the facts themselves—takes on a life of its own.

Whether the person who believes a lie is well meaning, maliciously inclined, ignorant, or self-delusive is not relevant. Truth is Stoic in nature; it doesn't concern itself with human intentions. Truth overwhelms everything and everyone in its path. In this respect, good intentions coupled with stupidity is a tragic mix of ingredients that has a tendency to lead to a view of the world as unjust.

As you move on to Chapter 2, remember that truth is the foundation of rational living, and that rational living is the foundation of happiness and success. Discovering truth involves courage, honesty, and, above all, a great deal of effort on your part. It must be *your* search for truth, no one else's. And, above all, be conscious of the fact that, because of its finiteness, there is an urgency to life. Therefore, getting sidetracked from truth for even a short period of time is certain to result in pain. No one

can go on believing whatever he wants to believe—creating his own reality—without suffering appropriate consequences. And if those consequences do not arrive until later in life, when the individual is ill-prepared to handle them, so much the worse.

If the prospect of middle- and old-age regret sounds painful to you, it should motivate you to start your search for truth as early as possible and to embrace it whenever and wherever you find it. When it comes to truth, the future is now. There will never be a better day than today to begin your search.

2

GET A LIFE

Principle #2: Focus on Value, Not Entitlements.

> I feel my heart glow with an
> enthusiasm which elevates me to
> heaven; for nothing contributes
> so much to tranquillise the mind
> as a steady purpose—a point on
> which the soul may fix its
> intellectual eye.
>
> DR. FRANKENSTEIN

There are two schools of thought about the future—fatalism and self-determination (determining your own destiny). While many people believe they have little or no control over how their lives play out, I strongly believe that you *can* have a great deal of control over your future by making independent, rational decisions that will result in your getting what you want.

For purposes of this book, the subject of fatalism versus self-determination constitutes far more than just an interesting intellectual discussion. Obviously, you can't work at making decisions that bring you long-term happiness if everything is predetermined.

Interestingly, there are both atheists and religionists who believe in fatalism. Many atheists believe that how the future unfolds (including the all-important distribution of genetic makeup) was predetermined by the nature of the Big Bang some 14 billion years ago. Many religious people, on the other hand, believe that God determines the course of events, which renders man impotent. In either case, while events may seem random to us, in reality they are predetermined by an outside force, either God or an inexplicable explosion, far too massive for us to comprehend, that occurred eons ago in the far reaches of space.

Of course, there is a middle ground for the religious person. He also can take the position that God predetermines some or most events, but not all, and that because man possesses free will, he can make choices that alter events that are not controlled by God. The problem is that he can never be certain as to which events are the domain of God and which ones are up for grabs. Thus, it may look like a contradiction when a seemingly self-reliant, positive person says things such as, "If it's meant to be, it's meant to be."

A fatalistic atheist can take an even more extreme view by seeing life as nothing more than an illusion. This view, known as "quietism," is based on the belief that there is no past, present, or future, and that what we perceive as the past, present, and future is nothing more than our mind playing tricks on us. In other words, the past, present, and future are illusions of our consciousness. If there is no future, of course, nothing can be changed, either by God or man. Quietism gives us a universe where everything is already in place—in other words, a dead universe. Thus, there is no point in trying to better our existence, because we have no future.

However, even if you're a total fatalist, I would argue, for practical reasons, that you still should make the effort to determine the outcome of your life. Your only other alternative is to merely pass the time until you cross into the next world, which certainly doesn't sound very stimulating. Also, in the event you're wrong, it would be a shame to realize it on your deathbed and regret not having taken control of your life when you had the opportunity to do so.

If you believe that only some things are predetermined, which is where I think most people stand, I would suggest that you not spend a lot of time worrying about which things are and which things are not beyond your control. It makes a lot more sense to pitch in and help God or the universe work His or its wonders. From whence comes the adage, "God helps those who help themselves."

In any event, the fact that you bought this book indicates that you are interested in bettering your life, so it's unlikely that you're a total fatalist. Making an effort to get what you want through rational living is simply not compatible with total fatalism.

IS THAT ALL THERE IS?

Whether or not you believe in extraterrestrial intelligence, the evidence for it certainly exists. In fact, I have long suspected that humanoids from another galaxy are walking among us, right here on planet Earth. These aliens apparently don't want to destroy us; they want only to enslave us to their benefit.

They appear to have organized a conspiracy that includes granting favors to terrestrial creatures who cooperate with them. The conspiracy revolves around a device whose purpose it is to dull our senses and steer us away from thoughts that might inspire us to better our existence. The code word for this device is *xobparc* (which, by coincidence, is *crapbox* spelled backward). Human beings have long referred to this insidious device as *television set*. An integral part of this conspiracy is that the aliens have entered into deals with the Japanese (to manufacture xob-parcs) and the television networks (to produce *eraf parc*—which, by another inexplicable coincidence, happens to be *crap fare* spelled backward). We humans have long referred to eraf parc as *television programming.*

Some of the more effective eraf parc that the television networks have created for the aliens include such artistic offerings as:

- Shuck and jive ads that tell us such intellectual things as, "The three most important words in the English language are, 'Hey, beer man!'" Or an ESPN ad that features a teenager mocking Tolstoy, sneering at the idea that some people suggest he should spend more time on schoolwork, and encouraging kids to pay more attention to what's happening on ESPN. These kinds of ads are not aimed at those who are already brain-dead; they are meant to entice only those who are still making an effort to resist that fate.

- The mindless chatter that is standard fare for daytime talk shows.

- Sitcoms so asinine that they insult the intelligence of grade-school kids.

- Nonstop college and professional sporting events, seven days a week, 365 days a year.

- Wrestling, *America's Funniest Home Videos*, cloned infomercials, and other assorted garbage.

To the untold millions of people who are entrapped in this kind of tragic existence, my compassionate side compels me to offer this piece of advice: Get a life! The first step toward determining your destiny is to escape, by any means necessary, the desensitizing eraf parc that is available twenty-four hours a day on your dreaded xobparc.

Allow me to be more specific: It means getting up out of your chair, *right now,* and emphatically saying, "No, I don't have to flood my brain with eraf parc today. I *do* have a choice."

But your xobparc is only one of the many mind-deadening temptations that continually beckon you. There are movies, amusement parks, live sporting events, social clubs masquerading as "health clubs," and daily treks to the fast-food killing machines. None of these activities, of course, can compare to spending endless hours in front of your xobparc and watching eraf parc, but all chip away at your limited time resources and prevent you from getting on with the serious and exciting business of life.

If any of this sounds at least vaguely familiar to you, it may be time for you to face the truth squarely in the eye. And the truth is that you can't expect to change your life for the better if you continue to spend inordinate amounts of time on frivolous activities. The fact that

> Rise above the
> walking dead.

you are surrounded by brain-dead people is no excuse. It's up to you to have the courage and self-discipline to rise above the walking dead.

REINCARNATION OF THE BRAIN

In the previous chapter, I wrote at some length about the danger of false premises that stem from faulty beliefs. The disintegration of Western culture over the past half-century has been the number-one culprit in encouraging people to harbor false premises, and at the top of the list is the phenomenon of victimization. All who embrace this pathetic notion are, at best, doomed to mediocrity.

If you're really serious about determining your own destiny and getting what you want in life, you must renounce the notion of victimization. It is a trap that has been set by vote-hungry politicians, self-anointed crusade leaders, and shameless legal hucksters operating under the respectable-sounding title of "personal injury attorney" (though I hasten to add that not all personal injury attorneys fall into this category). These master truth twisters spread lies that appeal to our human frailties, negatively condition our minds, and lead us to accept false premises.

There are two major problems with victimization. First, it allows a person to harbor the poisonous notion that material gain without work is possible. Second, those who capitalize on the victimization scam do so at the expense of others. Remember, if your intention is to search for truth, you must first love truth. You must love truth so much that you are willing to let go of cherished beliefs. Victimization is an area where it is especially easy to confuse truth with personal desires, and desires must always be subordinated to truth.

> Renounce the notion of victimization.

The acceleration of the victimization syndrome has reached such grotesque proportions that it now accords the *victim* label to virtually everyone. I have found nothing that deadens the soul—not even sitting in front of your xobparc hour after hour—quite like victimization. The first step, then, toward rising above a life of nothingness is to reject, in toto, the perverse concept of victimization. So long as you allow even a remnant of victimization to infiltrate your thinking processes, mental reincarnation is not possible. You first have to clean house in order to make room for constructive pursuits.

The Magic of Semantics

In order to eradicate the notion of victimization, it will be helpful if we back up a step and examine its roots. A human being is a creature of infinite desires, and it is quite normal to want to fulfill as many of those desires as possible. However, he is aware that

> Don't mistake wants
> for needs.

merely telling people he wants something is not likely to produce results. Thus, it has become popular to claim that whatever one desires is a "need." This transformation of a desire into a need is the first step toward victimization.

Need, quite obviously, is a subjective word; i.e., it is but an opinion. There is no such thing as an absolute need. I may think I need a Rolls-Royce; you may think I need a bicycle. Neither of us is right or wrong; we merely have a difference of opinion.

But my *desire* for a Rolls-Royce is another matter; there is no opinion involved there. If I desire a Rolls-Royce, that's my business. It only becomes your business if I arbitrarily decide that you have an obligation to buy it for me, on the grounds that it's a "need" and that I am therefore "entitled" to it. The fact that I may call my desire for a Rolls-Royce a *need* is, of course, semantic nonsense. I may just as well call it a wart, because regardless of what word I assign to it, I still have no moral right to force you to help me acquire it just because I happen to want it.

However, this camouflage is only the first step in the victimization semantics game. The second step involves the remarkable elevation of "needs" to "rights." All Western cultures now accept the belief that every individual has a "right" to an education, a "right" to a "decent" job, a "right" to a "minimum" wage, a "right" to "decent" housing, a "right" to virtually anything that a person can establish as "society's obligation" to him. This is quite a contrast to earlier times when most people believed that no one had a right to anything except life, liberty, and the pursuit of happiness.

Unfortunately, Western civilization has devolved to the point where the use of force and fraud can be easily justified on the grounds that such measures are necessary to make certain that people's "rights" are not violated, i.e., to make certain that their individual *desires* are fulfilled.

There is, quite obviously, one glaring problem with the desires-to-needs-to-rights game. In order to fulfill the "rights" of one person, another person's right to liberty must be violated, because any product or service that an individual may desire must be produced by someone else. And if the product or service (or the money to purchase it) is taken from a productive citizen against his will, then that citizen's rights are sacrificed to the desires of the person who receives the largesse.

Good news: You don't need a bushel full of artificial rights to get what you want in life. On the contrary, you can get everything you want—easier, faster, and in far greater abundance—without using government force to make others give it to you, and in the remainder of this chapter I will clearly spell out precisely how to do that. As a bonus, when you employ the honest, rational approach to getting what you want, your success gives you a sense of accomplishment and high self-esteem. If everyone got rewarded just for being alive, self-esteem would not be possible, and life would have no purpose.

PLAYING THE GAME

In case Americans think they have a monopoly on the rights game, allow me to pass along a bit of social perversity that is entrenched in New Zealand culture. In New Zealand, a job is an asset of the employee! The first time I heard this, I thought it was just a figure of speech, a way of expressing government extremism in protecting employees "rights." Not so; it is a literal fact.

I found this out the hard way when I started terminating employees at a company I owned in New Zealand. That's when, to my amazement, my solicitor told me that in order to do so, I had to detail the employee's misdeeds through copious note-taking over a long period of time. Further, I was required to spell out for the employee, in precise fashion, exactly what he was doing wrong. He recommended that I give the offending employee at least two letters to this effect over a period of about a month.

Worst of all is that attitude, which is number one on most

employer's lists when it comes to assessing an employee's value,
is not a valid reason for termination. If an employee's only crime
is that he is hateful and surly, poisoning the workplace atmosphere each day with his nasty attitude, you had better learn to
live with it for as long as he chooses to work for you.

Once you cross over the line and give an employee a warning
letter, it becomes a bit of a cat-and-mouse game, because the
employee is well aware that you intend to terminate him. This
gives him plenty of time to sabotage files, computers, and just
about anything else he thinks he can get his hands on without
getting caught. Of course, since you can't terminate him immediately, he also is in a position to bad-mouth you and your company to other employees.

Then, when the other shoe is dropped (i.e., termination
time), the game begins in earnest. The employee runs to a solicitor specializing in "labor relations"; the solicitor sends a letter
to the employer in which he demands, on behalf of the employee,
some outrageous number of months as termination pay; then the
employer responds with a much lower figure. Both parties fully
understand that it's just a game, and realize they will end up set-
tling somewhere in the area of three to twelve months, depending upon the employee's tenure. (If the employee has been
caught stealing, there is a chance that the settlement could be as
low as one month's severance pay. I'm not sure what the employer's financial obligation is in the case of first-degree murder.)

Sounds great for the victim-employee, right? Wrong. In reality, the job-is-an-asset-of-the-employee law is a hoax on New
Zealand employees. Why? Because it's such an outrageous law
that, as noted, it has evolved into a game. So employers, quite
naturally, do whatever they have to do to protect themselves.

First, the game has approximately the same effect on employment as minimum-wage laws. Employers simply hire as few
people as possible in order to reduce their risk. Second, they pay
the lowest possible wages in anticipation of the day when they

may have to terminate a worker, because termination pay is based on salary. So, in the end, what really happens is that an unemployed worker loses more income than he otherwise would as a result of less hiring, because on average he stays unemployed longer due to the job-is-an-asset-of-the-employee law. Then, when he finally lands a job, he earns a lower salary than he might otherwise earn, because the employer doesn't want to set himself up for a bone-crushing termination-pay settlement in the future.

When and if the employee is terminated, all the employer does, in effect, is give him back part of his losses in the form of severance pay. I say *part*, because I am convinced that an employee would be much ahead of the game financially if the government did not take the ludicrous position that he owns his job.

The Blame Game

Part and parcel to victimization is the Blame Game, a game in which people blame circumstances, conditions, or other people for their behavior and/or results. The Blame Game is at the wrong end of the accountability spectrum. It destroys self-esteem and confidence, and strips the afflicted individual of his motivation to solve his own problems.

In medical terminology, the Blame Game is known as *transference,* the act of looking to others, or to circumstances perceived to be beyond one's control, for the source of one's problems. In real terms, it means that the individual has conceded defeat, because he cannot solve problems over which he has no control. From the standpoint of living a rational life, it's almost analogous to brainwashing, though in the case of transference a person actually brainwashes himself. Remember, the integrity of your mind is sacred. Whether your thinking processes are violated by others or by your own erroneous beliefs is irrelevant. All other things being equal, either of these actions yields pretty much the same consequences.

Even when someone does something dishonest that causes you harm, you do yourself no favor by blaming your pain on him. There is a difference between engaging in transference and trying to analyze the reason you incurred a problem. There is always a *reason* for a bad consequence, but that's different from an *excuse*, the latter being a convenient way of escaping accountability. The fact that someone was dishonest with you could be a legitimate reason why you were harmed, but if you use the other person's dishonesty as an excuse for your problem, your reasoning powers are resting on quicksand.

You should therefore never release yourself from accountability, regardless of the circumstances. In other words, it's always in your best interest to look in the mirror for the cause of your problems. The guy looking back at you is the only person over whom you will ever have total control.

> Look in the mirror for the cause of your problems. The person looking back is the only one over whom you have total control.

In a case such as the one above, the best long-term solution for you is to learn from the bad experience and make it a point not to become involved with questionable people in the future, which is something that is to a great extent within your control. The best thing about the latter approach is that it isn't dependent upon your ability to get someone else to admit that he's in the wrong or to make reparations to you—which is good, because history teaches us that the possibility of either of these things happening is remote.

ALL THE KING'S MEN

I am reminded of a tale about a powerful king who called his wise men together and directed them to prepare a compilation of all the wisdom in the world. The wise men worked for many months, frantically researching and discussing a wide variety of subjects.

Finally, they presented the king with ten volumes of information that they were confident would please him.

The king perused a few pages of one volume, then said, "This is far too much material. Surely you can give me the wisdom of the world in less than ten volumes." So the king sent his wise men back to work on summarizing the wisdom contained in their ten volumes. Again, it took many months, but when they were done they had reduced their findings to a single volume.

Even more confident than the first time around, the wise men handed the king their work, whereupon he again perused a few pages. Shaking his head with dissatisfaction, he looked up and said, "Still far too much. I have no intention of reading all this material. Surely the wisdom of the world can be reduced to less than a volume."

The wise men, frustrated by the king's latest request, decided to go to extremes and reduce their findings to one page. This took them only about a month, and again they were confident that the king would be pleased. To their utter amazement, however, he was not. "Still too much material," bellowed the king. "What I want is the wisdom of the world summarized in *one sentence.*" The wise men gulped. How could all the wisdom of the world possibly be reduced to a single sentence?

The good thing about this seemingly impossible task was that they knew this had to be the end of the matter. Either they succeeded in accomplishing the seemingly impossible—summarize the wisdom of the world in one sentence—or be prepared to answer to a very angry king. The task proved to be daunting, to say the least, but, after considerable reflection and debate, they actually succeeded in condensing the one page into a single sentence.

Proudly, they approached the throne and said to the king, "Your majesty, we have at last summarized all the wisdom of the world in one sentence," whereupon the wisest of the wise men handed the king a single sheet of parchment. The king looked at the page before him, nodded his head approvingly, then read the sentence aloud:

THERE'S NO FREE LUNCH.

Sooner or later, we learn this truth and come to understand that there is a price for everything in life. There's a price for working hard; there's a price for not working hard enough. There's a price for saving for the future; there's a price for spending all your money now. There's a price for having children; there's a price for not having children. There's a price for having friends; there's a price for not having friends. There's a price for taking the right action; there's a price for taking the wrong action; and, yes, there's a price for taking no action at all.

In other words, you always have to give up something in order to get something in return. The empirical evidence suggests that even though most adults understand this principle on an intellectual level, they do not accept it on an emotional level. This results in actions that rational people describe as *irrational,* and irrational actions always produce bad consequences.

> There's a price for taking the right action; there's a price for taking the wrong action; and, yes, there's a price for taking no action at all.

Another way to describe price-paying is to view life as a never-ending series of trade-offs. No matter how attractive a person, a job, a deal, or a situation looks to you, make it a habit to open your eyes to the trade-offs. This is particularly important when something looks "too good to be true." Never forget that there's no such thing as a perfect person, a perfect job, a perfect deal, or a perfect situation.

Accepting the Unthinkable

Clearly, the wise men's summation of the wisdom of the world was 180 degrees removed from notions of victimization and government-created rights. This is also true of any and all other schemes and temptations to gain wealth without work. The reason I have never bought a lottery ticket is that I don't want to soil my belief system with hopes of striking it rich through pure luck. Lotteries are perhaps the ultimate free-lunch delusion, which is why they are a favored method of taxation by governments throughout the world. People who engage in self-delusion don't allow themselves to see the true nature of an insidious activity such as gambling.

The key to getting what you want is to think value instead of rights. You have no right to someone's love. You have no right to someone's friendship. You have no right to someone's respect. All these, and more, must be *earned,* and to the extent you create value for others, you will have them in abundance. Wealth, then, is a result of value creation, and because it is quantifiable it is an aspect of life that makes it easy for you to gauge how successful your efforts have been.

This is why it's a mistake to focus your life on making money. If you concentrate on value, money follows almost automatically. There is no mystery to this truth, for underlying it is a fundamental principle of human nature. The principle I'm referring to—let's call it the Selfishness Principle—is that human beings always attempt to do what they think is in their best interest. Or, put another way, people always make decisions that they believe will result in their experiencing the greatest amount of pleasure and least amount of pain.

Now, compare this to my definition of a rational life—the *conscious effort* to make *rational* decisions that result in an individual's getting what he wants *over the long term,* so long as the actions stemming from those decisions *do not involve the use of force or fraud against anyone else.* Note the words that have been left out of the Selfishness Principle. Most people don't make a *conscious effort* to make decisions, nor do they make *rational* decisions. Also, they don't often think *long term*. Worst of all, they don't think much one way or another about whether or not their actions involve *the use of force or fraud against anyone else.*

If you can't bear to accept the Selfishness Principle as a fact of life, ask yourself why millions of people buy foreign cars, notwithstanding the goading by auto manufacturers and auto workers for people to buy domestically produced automobiles. Not even government edicts and penalties can force people to stop buying better-quality foreign cars when given the opportunity to do so. The same is true of the garment industry, where garment workers' unions in most developed countries spend millions of dollars annually on advertising in an effort to cajole people into buying domestically produced garments instead of less expensive, often better-made, clothing manufactured in foreign countries.

If selfishness were not a reality of human nature, modern-day, multimillionaire professional athletes would gladly give part of their salaries to old-time superstars who paved the way for them. However, other than some gratuitous, nickel-and-dime funds targeted for totally destitute ex-players, today's wealthy athletes repeatedly vote against serious sharing of earnings with their predecessors who were so instrumental in making their wealth possible.

If you still doubt that people always attempt to act in their own best interests, try asking someone to buy your product just because you need the money. Trust me, you'll sleep a lot better at night if your success isn't dependent upon the altruistic nature of others. Where the marketplace is concerned, the reality is that consumers have no interest in a company's needs or problems. What they are interested in is what the company's products or services can do to make their lives more pleasurable or less painful, which is why it is so important to understand the truth about selfishness.

Thus, whether or not an individual lives a rational life, he always attempts to make decisions that he believes will result in his experiencing the greatest amount of pleasure and least amount of pain. In other words, the Selfishness Principle operates independently of our consciousness. That being the case, it is helpful to remember that principles cannot be created or altered; they can only be discovered. If your search for truth has been honest, you should have discovered this foundational principle of human nature long ago.

The late B. F. Skinner, collectivist psychologist and social theorist, spent his life searching for a scientific way to repress the human instinct to better one's existence. Skinner, by focusing on the modification of human behavior, was, in a de facto manner, acknowledging that self-interest is a natural and normal human characteristic. Only force can prevent human beings from acting in their own best interests.

Over the years, I have come to the conclusion that all disagreements regarding the subject of selfishness versus altruism are not really disagreements at all. Rather, they are a matter of semantics. If you help an old lady to cross the street, you do it for selfish reasons; i.e., because it makes you feel good. The self-styled moralist, however, insists that he performs the same deed out of sheer altruism. The fact is that your action and that of the moralist are one and the same; only the words (semantics) used to describe your actions are different.

When the moralist says that he helped an old lady cross the street, can he seriously deny that it made him feel good? I suppose he could split hairs and say that his good feeling was only a *result* of doing an unselfish deed, while your good feeling was the *intent* of your good deed. Well, first of all, the old lady doesn't give a hoot why either of you helped her; she's just happy to get to the other side of the street. Second, what's wrong with doing a good deed because it makes you feel good? Did Mother Teresa do her humanitarian work because it made her feel *bad?* Third, if the moralist really was thinking in altruistic terms, it wouldn't be

*"Knock off the altruism speech, fuzz ball,
and just get me across the street."*

so important to him to have to convince others that his good feelings came about only by accident. Fourth, his good feelings weren't by accident. Whether or not he consciously thought about it, he would not have helped the old lady cross the street if he didn't have good feelings about it.

Methinks what the moralist in this case really needs is a good shrink to analyze his childhood and comb out his obviously tangled neurons. The fact that there are so many tangled neurons in the world is why I

> Give others what they want
> in order to get what
> you want.

53

decided I could not, in good conscience, leave an explanation of selfishness versus altruism out of this book. If you've been conditioned to believe that selfishness is a bad thing, you already have two strikes against you when it comes to creating value, because without an understanding of selfishness you're likely to be unenthusiastic about value creation.

The fact that people are "selfish" is *why* you have to bring value to the marketplace. Giving others what *they* want selfishly motivates them to give you what *you* want. And a tough marketplace it is. In today's world of unlimited marketplace choices, the attitude of consumers is: So what? What's the big deal? Why should I buy your product? They are overwhelmed with offers and products, and, as a result, have become jaded. Therefore, if you're involved in selling a product—and virtually everyone is, even if the product is himself—you had better convince people in a hurry when it comes to selling them on the benefits of that product. An old marketing axiom says:

> *Tell me quick,*
> *And tell me true;*
> *Otherwise sir,*
> *To hell with you.*

In other words, if you want to sell someone on yourself or your product, you have to get to the point quickly. Tell the prospect everything that you or it will do for him, and don't waste his time with hyperbole. *Better, faster,* and *cheaper* are three magical words to remember when thinking about how to create value.

It's also crucial to realize that you can't sell people what you think they *should* want; consumers buy only what they *do* want. Likewise, value is *someone's else's* opinion of what your product or service is worth; your asking price is *your* opinion of what your product or service is worth. That being the case, never forget that customers aren't interested in your opinion. Thus, the virtue of selfishness in the marketplace is that no one can continue to produce a product if there aren't enough people who want to buy that product at the price that is being asked.

Thus, getting what you want in life is to a great extent about giving other people what *they* want.

When the Product Is You

Creating value is especially important when it comes to increasing your worth to an employer, or to individuals or companies in cases where you're selling your personal services. In this regard, always think of yourself as a product and recognize that a product with an enthusiastic, cooperative attitude has great value in the marketplace. Likewise, a product that turns out neat work has great value; a product that completes projects quickly has great value; and, above all, a product that can solve problems has great value. In fact, the surest way to get a promotion and pay raise is to be a problem solver. All employers need problem solvers, because all employers have problems. The greater the employer's problems, the greater the opportunities for problem solvers.

When I first moved to New Zealand, I inherited an office staff of thirteen after buying the New Zealand and Australian licensing rights to a line of health products. There's a lot of adjustment to living in a new country, so things were somewhat difficult in the early going. I couldn't seem to get anything done. I needed everything from paper clips to a new computer; I needed to get my files organized; I needed to put new policies and procedures in place. The list was endless.

Everyone in the office seemed to be working hard in his area of expertise, so I didn't want to take anyone away from his job to help me. However, there was a middle-aged woman (hereafter referred to as "Mary") who seemed to be functioning as a de facto office manager, and who looked as though she was knowledgeable about everything that was going on in the office. I noted that Mary's dress code was very professional and that she carried herself with a great deal of confidence. However, I also noted that she had a foreboding aura about her, seeming always to display an unpleasant expression.

Notwithstanding her perpetual frown, I thought Mary might be a good bet to become my executive assistant. Of course, before making such an offer to her I wanted to give her some tasks and see how well she performed them. Above all, I wanted to observe her attitude, as I have always placed a very high premium on attitude when it comes to assessing value.

One morning I buzzed Mary and asked her to come into my office, but, to my surprise, she said she was busy with some other important matters. She told me she would come to see me when she could break free. Several hours later, Mary finally came to my office and asked me what I had wanted. I told her that I would like to see how she handled some projects that I needed done, but I purposely did not tell her that I was thinking about the possibility of her becoming my assistant. I was aware of her salary, and was prepared to offer her a substantial pay raise if I felt confident she was right for the job, but I didn't want that fact to skew her performance.

Mary's response nearly took my breath away. Increasing the intensity of her perpetual scowl, she informed me that she already was overloaded with work and that she therefore would not be able to help me right now. Sure, Mary.

After catching my breath, I recalled some words of wisdom once passed along by Jerry Jones, owner of the Dallas Cowboys, in an interview. Said Jones, "If I have to remind an employee that I'm the boss, I've been doing something wrong." With this bit of inspiration lodged in my reptilian brain, the next day I was determined to be firm with Mary. I decided to go to her office and tell her that I wanted to see her immediately. I was getting further behind in my work every day, and was becoming ever more desperate for help. Notwithstanding Mary's self-destructive attitude, I made up my mind that I was going to help her turn things around—for her sake and mine.

As I began to walk out of my office, Mary happened to be rushing past my door. Instinctively, I raised my hand, right index finger pointed upward, and said, in a pleasant, almost deferential tone, "Oh, Mary, could I see you for a moment in my office?" She never even looked back, choosing instead to continue walking briskly toward her demise. Waving a hand over her shoulder in a brush-aside manner, she retorted, "I can't talk now. I'm very busy." Sure, Mary.

At this point, considering the somewhat aggressive thoughts running through my mind, I found myself thinking about how lucky I was that New Zealand had outlawed capital punishment. I was concerned that if much more time passed without my taking action, Mary might end up asking me if I would like to be *her* assistant. Antiquated laws aside, now I was *really* getting desperate to find someone to help me. Convinced that no one else in the office was right for the job, I was on the verge of giving up and submitting to the masochistic ordeal of working with an employment agency to fill my needs.

Then, figuratively speaking, a funny thing happened on the way to the employment agency. As I passed through the reception room on the way to my office the next morning, I routinely said hello to the receptionist, a young lady who was generally thought to be an airhead. What struck me on that particular morning was her smile—a wide, toothy grin that might best be described as an affidavit smile. I couldn't help but note the contrast to Mary's trademark frown.

Impulsively, I asked, "Joanne, how would you like to do a couple of projects for me this morning?" To which she immediately responded, "I'd *love* to, Mr. Ringer." I had her follow me to my office, then handed her a stack of newspaper tear sheets containing an advertisement that our company had just run. "I'd like you to fold each of these tear sheets neatly into quarters, put them in a pile with all of them facing in the same direction, then bring them back to me as soon as possible," I instructed.

I had given out many test projects such as this over the years, the object being to (1) observe the individual's attitude with regard to my asking for both neatness and speed, (2) see how quickly she completed the project, and, above all, (3) determine how literally she interpreted the word *neatly*. In Joanne's case, she immediately and enthusiastically responded, "No problem. I'll take care of this right away." In much less time than I anticipated, she returned to my office and proudly placed the pile of tear sheets on my desk. They were folded precisely as I had requested and stacked up perfectly. As you probably guessed, the next thing out of her mouth was, "Is there anything else I can do for you, Mr. Ringer?"

As you also probably guessed, I hired her on the spot as my

executive assistant. Happily, her attitude and skills turned out to be far better than I ever could have imagined. Joanne, the twenty-one-year-old airhead receptionist whom no one in the office had taken seriously, proved to be one of the brightest people who had ever worked for me. Skills and training? They didn't matter, because she was so bright and enthusiastic, so teachable, that she picked things up more quickly than anyone with whom I had ever worked. Throw in loyalty beyond the call of duty, and I guess you'd have to call her the draft pick of the century.

Watching Joanne grow over the years has been a source of great delight for me. Today, she is mature and highly skilled, and as enthusiastic as she was during her first encounter with me. But when she initially became my assistant, the office staff didn't know what to make of the situation. Image is a fascinating thing. Imagine one day having a perception of a person as a know-nothing receptionist, and the next day seeing her as assistant to the executive chairman. Luckily, notwithstanding the staff's misperceptions of her, Joanne was ready to assume serious responsibility from the outset. Within a matter of months, she took full control of the office and got things into the exact shape I wanted. Her forte, as you would imagine, was problem solving.

As for Mary, well, she wasn't thrilled with how events unfolded. I was told that for some time she kept a Joanne doll at home, but had eventually dismembered it and tossed the body parts into her fireplace.

Many months later, when I finally set in motion Mary's inevitable termination, she said to me, her finest scowl perfectly in place, "I know you've never liked me and that you've been trying to get rid of me from the very beginning." My initial impulse was to tell her that, on the contrary, what I really had been hoping to do from the outset was promote her to the position of assistant to the executive chairman and give her a substantial pay raise, but that she couldn't seem to find time to discuss the matter with me. I even thought about trying to explain to her that it would be much to her advantage if she worked on changing her unpleasant attitude and concentrated on ways to create value for whomever her next employer might be.

Instead, I mumbled a few meaningless, formal sentences, wished her luck, and told her to have her solicitor call me so we could begin playing the settlement game. The reason I didn't tell Mary what I was really thinking was that I knew her well enough by then to be convinced that the truth was the last thing in the world she would want to hear. It didn't take a master's degree in psychology to be pretty certain that Mary had experienced problems with every job she had had, and that she was a per-

> Surround yourself with problem solvers, not problem creators.

son with a desperate need to practice transference in order to avoid the unthinkable task of searching for truth in her own mirror. I wondered how many other employers in her past had heard her accuse them of not liking her and wanting to get rid of her. Worst of all for Mary, how many *future* employers would eventually hear the same transference words coming from her lips?

In simple terms, Joanne created value by understanding how to solve problems; Mary understood only how to create problems.

PASSIONATE ANTICIPATION

Creating value may be the key to success, but it doesn't do you any good just to talk about it. Attitude is to value creation as water is to a garden, because value tends to grow in direct proportion to attitude. Volumes have been written about the importance of attitude as it relates to success and happiness. In fact, the subject has been so dissected by so many thousands of writers and speakers that the term *positive attitude* has become something of a cliché. Nonetheless, it's a subject that doesn't fade away like last year's fad. On the contrary, it transcends the ages.

If you happen to be a doubter when it comes to the power of

> Value grows in direct
> proportion to attitude.

positive thinking—as I was for many years—consider a corollary of sorts: How many times have you achieved successful results when you were in a *negative* state of mind? If success is synonymous with failure avoidance, then negative thoughts should be at the top of your list of things to avoid. Can you imagine the results of introducing yourself to the woman of your dreams and thinking, "I know she's going to think I'm a worm. I shouldn't even try, because I'm just going to make a fool of myself." You'd need one of the great opening lines in history to overcome that kind of mind-set.

Attitude is no longer the exclusive domain of self-help speakers and writers. Increasingly, it is being studied by serious researchers and discussed at universities worldwide. The idea of changing your life by changing your thoughts is a stunning notion that a clear majority of the population now believes, though most people fail to put it into practice on a consistent basis. Further, the fact that it is within your power to change your thoughts makes the concept that much more remarkable. Best of all, short of outright physical force, no one can make you abandon your mental state.

Can you transform a thought into a physical reality? Scientific evidence clearly suggests that you can. Studies conducted by Dr. Karl Pribram, a Stanford University neurosurgeon, have shown that by holding sharp images in the mind, a person can influence his results in just about any endeavor he undertakes—from getting a good grade on an exam to winning an athletic contest to making money. What appears to happen is that a clear mental image stimulates the various body mechanisms to do whatever is necessary to convert that image into a physical reality. These body mechanisms draw to the person the things, people, and circumstances necessary for him to accomplish his objectives.

The body mechanisms I am referring to go far beyond the obvious ones such as sight, hearing, and sensory perception. I believe that what underlies the thoughts-to-physical-reality phe-nomenon is that all atoms on earth—and, indeed, throughout the universe—are connected. If one accepts this premise, it log-ically follows that what happens to the atoms in your brain has an effect on atoms outside your body. We know that atoms vi-brate at tremendous speeds, so whether they give off positive or negative energy is of monumental importance.

In fact, it is very possible that distance is not a major factor when it comes to atoms affecting one another. This, I believe, is why so many people have reportedly had telepathic experiences with family members, friends, or acquaintances thousands of miles away, or even on the other side of the world. On a number of occasions, I have had the experience of someone calling me on the phone for the first time in many months at the very moment I was thinking of him, even though I, in turn, had not had him on my mind for a very long period of time. Does anyone possess the knowledge to dispute the possibility that atoms have an unquan-tifiable power to transcend distance? I think not, which is why I believe it makes good sense to accept the empirical evidence in an area that can be so crucial to determining one's destiny.

It logically follows that the more specific the image, the more powerful and stimulating that image is when it comes to affect-ing other atoms. After winning an Olympic gold medal, U.S. de-cathlon champion Dan O'Brien explained, "The decathlon takes place in your mind first. If I didn't wake up thinking I was going to win the gold medal—or set a world record—I wouldn't. I con-trol my own destiny." I like to think of this phenomenon as "pas-sionate anticipation," a passion for what one believes the future holds.

Alexander Graham Bell, with somewhat stronger credentials than I, shared his thoughts on this subject by saying, "What this power is I cannot say; all I know is that it exists and it becomes available only when a man is in that state of mind in which he knows exactly what he wants and is fully determined not to quit until he finds it."

Of course, even when you have a positive attitude, it's still possible for things to work out badly, but what's to be gained by being negative? When you think about it, then, a sufficient reason for concentrating on positive thoughts is that it's an everything-to-gain-and-nothing-to-lose proposition.

Checking Inventory

A good attitude is instrumental in creating value, and it is the creation of value that gives you the best chance of getting what you want. But what if you lack the right attitude? One of the most frequently asked questions in letters I have received over the years is, "How can I motivate myself if I'm not naturally motivated?" In other words, how can I change my attitude? It's a fair question. You do, indeed, have to be motivated to change your attitude and thus create value.

Can you fake motivation? Sure, and if you're really good at it, you should be able to fool most people for at least twelve minutes. But it isn't a question of fooling others; it's a question of *experiencing* the kind of motivation that results in value creation. And what fuels motivation is passion, passion so strong that you become relentless in pursuit of an objective. So the real question is, how do you develop passion?

If you came home one day and found your house in flames and your family trapped inside, you would probably develop an instant passion so strong that you would try to make your way through the flames in an effort to save your family. What would cause such an instant passion is *purpose*. Your purpose—i.e., your objective—would be instantly clear. It also would be clear to you that time was a limiting factor, thus you would spring into action without feeling the necessity to do a lot of research or enter into a prolonged discussion with anyone else about the matter.

If I saw you working with this kind of passion in a business setting, I'd probably offer you just about anything to persuade you to join my team. Of course, it's unlikely that you could ever be as passionate about business as you would be when trying to save the lives of your family, but it's certainly a good goal to shoot for. Why? Because the closer you can come to duplicating that kind of passion in other aspects of your life, the more likely you are to create value. So the next question becomes, how do you find an occupation, business, venture, or career about which you can become passionate?

The last thing in the world you want to do is mistake speed for direction, because if your emphasis is on speed alone, you could be moving sideways. Worse, you could be moving backward. That's why you should avoid the temptation to jump into the first opportunity that comes along, especially if it has a get-rich-quick aura about it. To be sure, history has had its share of pet-rock success stories, but for the most part, history has repeatedly demonstrated that gimmicks are not a good bet. Creating legitimate value is the straightest line between where you are now and where you want to be. It doesn't matter how fast or how hard you work if your efforts don't create value for others.

In this regard, the first step toward creating value is to take an honest, internal inventory. Think long and hard about your abilities and deficiencies. Just as important, recognize that you have a much better chance of getting what you want in life by working at something you enjoy, so this is an area where a search for truth is crucial. You have to be brutally honest with yourself when answering these questions, so take plenty of time to think about them, preferably in quiet solitude.

You also should be careful about discussing your abilities and deficiencies with others, and even more careful when it comes to deciding what activities you most enjoy. Remember, what I'm talking about here is your life, and your decisions regarding these issues might very well determine how you spend the remainder of that life. No one, not even a spouse, knows as much about you as you do.

Many young people fall into the trap of doing something

temporarily just to make money, with the intention of doing what they really want to do later on when their financial condition is more stable. Billionaire Warren Buffet put this kind of logic into proper perspective in an interview with *Fortune* magazine when he said, "I get to do what I like to do every single day of the year. . . . It's tremendous fun. . . . I always worry about people who say, 'I'm going to do this for ten years; I really don't like it very well. And then I'll do this. . . .' That's a little like saving up sex for your old age. Not a very good idea."

Creating value, then, stems from passion; passion stems from belief in what you're doing; belief in what you're doing (i.e., a purpose) stems from working at something you not only are good at, but enjoy. When you get all these factors going in the right direction, you have no trouble being motivated to do whatever it takes to succeed. There is nothing quite so exhilarating as working yourself to the point of exhaustion for months, or even years, then being handsomely rewarded for your efforts in the marketplace. Every human being should treat himself to this drug-free high at least once in his lifetime.

THE URGENCY FACTOR

I don't recall where I first heard the following parable, but it certainly is profound and appropriate to any discussion about creating value.

> *Every morning in Africa, a gazelle wakes up. It knows that it*
> *must run faster than the fastest lion or it will be killed.*
> *Every morning in Africa, a lion wakes up. It knows that it*
> *must run faster than the slowest gazelle or it will starve.*
> *It doesn't matter whether you are a lion or a gazelle. When the*
> *sun comes up, you had better start running!*

As human beings, we find that we, too, had better start running at the crack of dawn if we're serious about achieving our goals. A stress-free life sounds nice in theory, but in reality there is an inherent urgency to life. First, life is finite, and you don't even have the advantage of knowing when your finite supply of time will run out. Second, life is competition. No matter what the situation, you're always competing with other human beings. You compete for a prospective spouse, you compete for a place on an athletic team, you compete for attention from others, you compete every day of your life in numerous ways you don't even think about.

Above all, you have to compete in the marketplace, whether you're selling a product, a service, or yourself as an employee or prospective employee. It's not good enough just to create value. In today's hi-tech, fast-changing world, you have to create value *quickly.* If not, your product or service will rapidly lose its worth. An obvious example of this is the computer world. At the rate both software and hardware companies have fallen behind the times since personal computers first exploded onto the scene in the late 1970s, Computer Heaven may soon have to rent more space.

I recall two companies, Wang and Xerox, that were early leaders in the computer field. They didn't produce computers per se, but, rather, dedicated word processors. Xerox produced a tank-sized machine called the Xerox 860, with an operating system that had to be reloaded each morning. Wang's machines looked much more like today's modern computers, and were far quieter than the Xerox 860. For a long time, it seemed as though every office you visited had either Xerox or Wang word processors, and the two companies appeared to be way out front in the computer market.

However, led by Apple, the rest of the industry was moving toward multitask computers, and word processing was just one feature of these much more sophisticated machines. Xerox, whose arrogance is legendary in the world of big business, ignored "kids" like Steven Jobs and Bill Gates, feeling confident that its customers would remain loyal. Naively, it didn't understand the Selfishness Principle—that human beings always attempt to do what they think is in their own best interest. When Xerox finally woke up, it was too late. I got rid of my last Xerox 860 in the mid-1980s, years after it had been taking up too much space in my garage. Because its value had fallen to zero, I had to pay someone to take it away.

With Wang, it appeared to be more a matter of ignorance than arrogance—though the two seem to go hand in hand—and the result was worse than that of Xerox. After years of floundering, the company finally ousted the founder's son from his CEO position and ultimately filed for bankruptcy. It's yet another reminder that when it comes to a search for truth, you can always count on stupidity overriding good intentions. Wang later tried to revive itself in selected countries, but it was far too late. When it finally peeked out of its cave, it gazed at a brave new world dominated by strange names like Microsoft, Compaq, and Apple.

Dead on Arrival

Through firsthand experience, I can attest to how quickly products lose their value in the rapidly changing world of computers. After years of untold wasted hours poking around in WordPerfect just enough to get by, I reluctantly came to the conclusion that if I wanted to speed up my writing output, I was going to have to invest the time to gain an in-depth understanding of the program.

Meanwhile, my assistant, Joanne, had been trying to get me to switch to Microsoft Word. However, like most people who know just enough to barely get by on a computer, I was insecure about letting go of the one software program I could dabble around in and actually manage to turn out a semi-acceptable document.

Finally, with considerable apprehension, I decided to go along with Joanne's recommendation, and we switched all of our office computers to Word. What helped push me over the line was Joanne's assurances that all I would need was a good Word reference guide and I'd be up and running in no time.

Being the kind of person who likes to cover all the bases, I didn't buy just one reference guide—I bought eight. Which only served to make my disappointment eight times greater. Not only did I find it difficult and time-consuming to search for answers to my questions in these reference guides, but even when I succeeded in finding the information I was searching for, the instructions usually proved to be confusing. I was convinced I had given new meaning to the term *computer illiterate*.

Given that the majority of computer users do their word processing with Word, it was difficult to understand why no one had thought to create a true reference guide on the subject, something resembling a dictionary or thesaurus wherein the user could look up answers in alphabetical order. Since I could find nothing remotely close to this concept in bookstores, I decided that the only way I was going to have such a resource at my disposal was to create it myself.

Through a combination of lessons, studying, and endless hours of trial and error, I became what could loosely be referred to as a "Word expert." As time passed, I began sharing my homemade reference guide with friends and business associates, and their enthusiastic comments were quite flattering. In fact, many of them urged me to expand my customized "book" and make it available to the general public. I finally decided to take them up on their suggestion, because, based on my own experience, I was convinced that the concept I had created could be of tremendous value to Microsoft Word users.

The project involved nearly two years of detailed, exhausting work, but the result seemed worth it—a 656-page book I dubbed *Wordasaurus Quick-Answer Guide: The System for Mastering Microsoft Word*. My concept was much like learning a foreign language while living in another country; i.e., a user could become adept

"Please, Mr. Gates, don't turn me away.
I'll promise to testify on your behalf."

at Word while doing his normal, day-to-day work. There was no doubt in my mind that I had created a valuable resource.

One problem: I had vastly underestimated the impact of how quickly Microsoft upgraded its software (on average every eighteen-to-twenty-four months). The *Wordasaurus Quick-Answer Guide* was based on Microsoft Word 95, Version 7, which most people were using when I had started the project. But by the time my book came off the press, most users had moved on to Word 97, and, worse, Microsoft was beginning to talk about Word 2000. After two years of hard labor, I was facing the prospect of two more years to create a book on Word 2000—just in time for Microsoft to release Word 2002! Not being attracted to masochism, I decided to pass.

My painful experience was a grim reminder of how big a factor urgency is in the marketplace, no matter how much value one creates. Never forget that value is perishable. It's a grave mistake to fall so in love with a project that it prevents you from moving quickly enough. The best laid plans of mice and men are sometimes dead on arrival.

Also, keep in mind that the economic marketplace is not the only area of life where urgency is a factor. The earth, the universe, and life itself are in a perpetual state of change. To the degree you do not anticipate change and take necessary action, you will end up *reacting* to life's inevitable changes, which means you'll be dealing from a position of weakness. Proactive people are almost always in a stronger position than reactive people.

In the little anecdote I related earlier about how Joanne became my assistant, she took swift action to demonstrate her value. Had she been as cavalier as Mary, I might have hired another assistant through an employment agency, at which point Joanne's potential value to me would have dropped dramatically. To the extent the new assistant created value, Joanne's value would have dropped even more. Repeated personal experience has convinced me that time is of the essence when it comes to creating value.

Clearly, then, a major component of getting what you want in life is to create value for others, and create it with an urgency that respects life's never-ending changes.

3

CHARACTER OF THE SOUL

Principle #3: Make Choices with Civility, Divinity, Honesty, and Humility.

> There are nine hundred and
> ninety-nine patrons of virtue
> to one virtuous man.
>
> **HENRY DAVID THOREAU**

Most of us have been socialized to believe that we will get what we want in life by working hard at our jobs, but it rarely occurs to us that it's equally important to work hard at making ourselves into better human beings. Achievement in business, love, friendship, or any other area of life does not precede personal growth; it follows it. It's very important not to attempt to reverse the order of this principle. What I'm referring to is "personal infrastructure," the virtues that make you what you are. The sum total of your virtues is what gives character to your soul. No matter how great a person's success in other areas of life, a weak personal infrastructure is certain to result in pain.

A strong personal infrastructure, on the other hand, is a virtually certain way to increase pleasure.

There are two issues involved here. The first is how others perceive you (and remember you after you're gone); the second is what you really are inside. How others perceive you may affect the quality of your daily life, but it cannot affect the character of your soul. However, the foundation of every civilization is a generally accepted code of conduct, and within the framework of the civilization of which you are a part, the reality is that you are judged by others. Further, it is human nature to want others to perceive you in a positive light. You are judged first by how you look; second, by what you say; third, and most important, by your actions.

What you do to embellish your physical appearance—from wardrobe to hair style—has both a short- and long-term impact on how others perceive you. On the other hand, your *natural* physical appearance—i.e., wardrobe and hair style aside— is not a problem. Think of the ten people whom you most admire. Is your admiration for any of these people based on how good-looking they are? Undoubtedly, you admire these people for their accomplishments and/or character.

> How much people need you depends upon how much value you offer them. Trust and respect lead to added value.

As to what you say and how you act, you should always keep in mind that to get what you want in life, you need three things from people: You need them to trust you; you need them to respect you; and you need them to place a high value on what you have to offer. We thoroughly covered value in the last chapter, so suffice it to say that how much people need you depends upon how much value you offer them.

How much people trust and respect you, however, goes far beyond creating value. Trust and respect translate into *added* value; thus, they have the potential to elevate a modest success into a super success. They are common currencies that can be spent in virtually every country. A person halfway around the globe who trusts you is an asset; a person in your own town who distrusts you is a liability. When your distrust liabilities begin to pile up, your value diminishes in the marketplace.

Of course, you could argue that a person can fake virtues in order to win people over, and short term that's probably true. Long term, however, virtues cannot be faked any more than can attitude. Thus, consistency ultimately rules the day. Consistency, in a moral sense, is a synonym for integrity, i.e., adherence to high moral principles. A person who consistently acts in accordance with such principles is thought of as *ethical.* A person who preaches a high standard of morality, but selectively acts otherwise (situational ethics) is thought of as *hypocritical.* "Social conscience" groups that have no qualms about resorting to violence to further their causes are notorious examples of hypocrisy.

The first step toward acting ethically is to think ethically. It's not about "walking the talk"; it's about walking the thought. In other words, it's your day-in-day-out thoughts that determine the character of your soul, because actions automatically follow thoughts.

A human being is the only matter on this planet whose atoms are arranged in such a way that it can reflect on its very existence. Perhaps the most important difference between man and animals is that an animal knows, but a man knows that he knows. We can therefore choose to change the nature of our existence, and the starting point for all such change is from within. Fortunately, we all pretty much agree on which traits are virtuous—such things as patience, understanding, kindness, compassion, graciousness, and perseverance, to name but a few. We agree because, modern-day relativism aside, certain things "feel right" and certain things "feel wrong." It feels right to be

> The first step toward acting ethically is thinking ethically.

gracious; it feels right to be kind; it feels right to be compassionate. Can anyone seriously debate this?

In the remainder of this chapter, I am going to discuss four virtues from which I believe most other virtues stem—civility, dignity, honesty, and humility. To achieve the trust and respect of others, vigilance in these areas is crucial. More important, however, is that these virtues result in self-respect, and self-respect is an important ingredient in getting what you want in life.

CIVILITY

Recently, I felt like doing something outrageous, so I stopped at an ice cream shop in a nearby strip mall. Inside was a familiar scene: Rock music blasting in the background, a young man behind the counter with long, unkempt blond hair, and a group of pals hanging around and gabbing with him. After waiting a couple of minutes for the young man to begrudgingly excuse himself from his social obligations, he turned to me and snarled, "Yeh?" (His version of "May I help you?")

"I'd like a chocolate chip cone, please," I said. Without so much as a grunt, he inserted two dirty fingers inside a cone and carried it over to the ice cream containers. Then, with his unwieldy hair dangling into the chocolate chip ice cream, he proceeded to mash a dip of ice cream onto the cone, wipe his nose with the back of his right hand while handing me my ice cream cone with his left hand, and mumble, "Here ya go." (His version of "Here's your ice cream cone, sir.")

Trying hard not to show my nausea, I paid for the cone, walked outside, and tossed it into the first trash container I came to. So much for doing something outrageous.

About a block from the mall, I saw through my rearview mirror a pickup truck bearing down on me. Not just any old pickup truck, but one of those silly-looking getups where the body sits atop tires that look like they were made for a 747 aircraft. As the driver began pounding away on his horn in an effort to get me to

hit the gas and exceed the speed limit, I tapped my brake a couple of times to keep him from rear-ending me. The punk kid behind the wheel almost went berserk. He put the truck in overdrive and came roaring up beside me. With ball cap dutifully worn in the "up yours" backward position and iridescent-rim sunglasses firmly in place, he shouted a remarkable array of obscenities and flipped me the obligatory bird.

Finally, I arrived home. Now I could relax and lock out the insanities of the modern world. I turned on the television set, only to be greeted by some rude, foul-mouthed weirdos who were expounding on their "rap philosophy" for an interviewer. Employing my weapon of last resort—the remote control—I quickly zapped the rappers.

The evening news would be safe. A reporter was talking to a guy in his early twenties adjacent to his car. The reporter, noting that the young man's car radio had been loudly blasting rock music at an intersection, wanted to know what he thought of a proposed law that would make it illegal to play your car radio at a level that could be heard beyond ten feet. His answer was stimulating: "Ah figure it's mah right to play mah radio as loud as ah please, and if the guy next to me don' like it, he kin jus' roll up his winda and hang a hard right." Peace-loving soul that I am, thoughts of the death penalty for car-radio blasting flashed through my mind.

Two Excedrins later, I again changed channels. Aha! Just what I needed—*The Jerry Springer Show.* The topic today was married couples with gay lovers. What more could I ask for? With thoughts of capital punishment again dancing through my head, I called up a philosopher friend of mine, hoping to get some reassurance that I was overreacting. Thankfully, he pontificated on how the world is always in the process of changing, and that what appears to be offensive today will probably be considered mild by tomorrow's standards. Whew—what a relief. And here I thought there was something fundamentally wrong with Western culture.

Satisfied that all was well, I leaned back in my easy chair and reflected on how lucky we are. A man can relax in his home without worry, knowing that there are whole armies of people out there to protect us. The ACLU fights for our right to say and do anything that happens to suit our fancy. Nader's Raiders protect us from the evils of big business. And, above all, we don't need to worry about dangerous people harming us, because we have federal prosecutors to put uncivilized monsters like Michael Milken and Leona Helmsley in jail.

I felt such a sense of security that I even thought about going back and trying for another ice cream cone. I decided against it, however, when I began picturing strands of dirty blond hair stuck in my intestines. Besides, being the considerate person I am, I didn't want to be responsible for once again interrupting the teen-babble session that the kid behind the counter was having with his pals.

PEOPLE OFTEN get discouraged by the moral decline of Western civilization, and there's certainly good reason for such discouragement—young people who rarely give up their seats to adults on a bus or subway, bare-chested, obnoxious fans who have taken over most sports stadiums, and movies that offer foul language, explicit sex, and stomach-turning violence, to name but a few examples.

The good news, however, is that you can choose not to succumb to the madness of the crowd. You can't do a great deal to stop the decadence that surrounds you or to change the morality of society as a whole, but that doesn't mean that you have to contribute to it. Achieving happiness is not about altering society; it's about you—the only person who can totally control the character of your soul. In today's world of rudeness and impudence, courteous and polite people may seem like anachronisms, but they command the admiration and respect of those who matter most—other civilized people.

> Courteous and polite people command true admiration and respect of those who matter most—other civilized people.

DIGNITY

As my first book rose to the top of the bestseller lists, I was invited to appear on most of the major talk shows. *The Tonight Show* was considered to be the pinnacle for authors, so when I finally got the opportunity to be a guest on the show, I was quite excited. A ten-minute stint on the *The Tonight Show* could sell thousands of books.

This was early in my career, and I was not aware that talk-show producers are primarily interested in guests who have what is commonly referred to in the business as a *shtick*. Shtick can be almost anything that makes a guest stand out from the norm, the more outrageous the better.

Today, the shtick of choice is sexual deviation of one kind or another. At that time, however, just having written a book with the shocking title of *Winning through Intimidation* was good enough to qualify. On meeting the talent coordinator, he warned me that the producer didn't like boring guests, and that I should "play up the intimidation thing real big." I felt an uneasiness about the idea, but mentally waived it aside. Instead, like the obedient little tortoise I was, I assured him that it would be no problem.

When the night of my scheduled appearance finally arrived, the same feeling of uneasiness returned. While waiting to be called as a guest, I felt as though something just wasn't right, but before I could get too deeply into my thoughts I was told it was my turn to go on stage. I was whisked away by a bearded young chap in faded blue jeans, led though a maze of bland corridors, and told to stand behind the stage curtain until my name was called.

As soon as the guest host, McLean Stevenson, bellowed my name, I came bouncing out from behind the curtain in my best Hollywood stride and made my way to the guest's chair. Right off the bat, Stevenson asked, "So tell me, how do you intimidate people?" I smiled outwardly, but inside I winced, because my book was not about how to intimidate people. It was about how to mount a *defense* against the words and actions of intimidating people, which was 180 degrees removed from the question Stevenson had posed.

Repressing my discomfort, I put on my best shtick face and said, "Well, for example, the fact that you're sitting behind that desk on a raised platform is a very good setting for employing in-timidation." Whereupon Stevenson got out of his chair and said, "Heck, if that's what it takes, *you* sit behind the desk and I'll be *your* guest." The crowd roared its approval as though it were about to witness a mud-wrestling event between two midget transvestites. I could feel my shtick gears turning faster and faster inside me. Play my cards right and, who knows, I could become another Richard Simmons.

I jumped up from my chair, stepped onto the raised platform, and seated myself in the host's chair. With the audience still drowning itself in laughter, Stevenson challenged me, "Okay, babe, now it's *your* show. Let's see some intimidation."

Hard as it is to believe today, I smoked an occasional cigar during that period of my life, and I happened to have one in my pocket. Realizing that I needed to quickly come up with a good piece of shtick in order to reinforce the image that the producer

"Okay, babe, now it's your show. Let's see some intimidation."

and Stevenson wanted me to project, I whipped the cigar out of my breast pocket, slowly and with great drama peeled off the cellophane wrapper, stuck the cigar in my mouth, and lit it up with a napalm-size flame from my cigarette lighter.

I thought the audience's reaction couldn't get any louder, but when I proceeded to blow a smoke ring in Stevenson's direction, pandemonium broke out. Thoughts of running for president (of the National Association of Clowns, Bozos, and Criminal-Defense Attorneys) shot through my mind. Could it get any better than this? With good enough shtick, anything might be possible!

Being high on shtick is like no other drug, because it doesn't abuse your body in any way. What it does do, however, is abuse your self-esteem. Shtick is at the far (i.e., wrong) end of the dignity spectrum. After the show, as I started to awaken from my trance, sanity began to grip me. An annoying little voice from deep within my brain admonished, "You, sir, have just made an ass of yourself in front of 10 million people."

In the days that followed, I had a severe shtick hangover. I couldn't look in the mirror. My performance not only was undignified, it was dishonest. I had led a nationwide audience to believe that my book was about how to intimidate people, which it most definitely was not. I had compromised my integrity to play a role that was expected of me by others. Short term, it was at first exhilarating, then humiliating. Long term, however, it was one of the most beneficial things that ever happened to me, because I never forgot the experience. My vigilance about maintaining my dignity at all costs remains to this day, and I am especially wary of people who want me to present an artificial persona.

THE EMBARRASSING LITTLE TALE I just related underscores how easy it is to compromise one's dignity. Dignity is an essential element of happiness, because it gives you self-respect, a commodity that in turn gives you the confidence you need to achieve your goals. Nevertheless, dignity is a rare commodity in our bizarre, modern-day world. We see confirmation of this all around us, such as:

- Talk shows that feature tragic people who emotionally and psychologically disrobe themselves in public while sharing their most intimate thoughts with millions of strangers.

- Attorneys who routinely advertise on television, radio, and even billboards, urging prospects to demand their rights through legal action, though not that many years ago such actions would have resulted in an attorney's being disbarred.

- A tidal wave of verbal sloth. The "F word" has long been the *in word,* especially among teenagers. Worse, news commentators on the major networks routinely use incorrect words and phrases such as *"very* unique" (unique means *one of a kind*), *ir*regardless (no such word), and "he is a man *that* always finishes" (*who* always finishes). And, of course, the word "like" is inserted in front of virtually every sentence, as in, "Like, I mean, what am I supposed to do?"

- Doctors and other professionals who wear casual clothes, even blue jeans, to the office.

- Role-model, multimillionaire athletes who fill mind-dulling interviews with meaningless, trite comments such as, "That's what it's all about."

- Millions of people worldwide who surrender their individuality and throw in their lots with political-action groups who demand their "rights" (i.e., insist that government fulfill their desires at the expense of others).

Dignity is not a finite subject, because there are endless ways in which a person can lose his dignity: chasing after people who do not show him respect, kowtowing to the wealthy and powerful, or just acting childish. With regard to the latter, I recall Tony Bennett saying in an interview, after Frank Sinatra died, that the best piece of advice Sinatra had given him was to not sing silly songs if he wanted to be around for a long time. Silliness doesn't wear well on adults, so be on guard against people who encourage you to act like a clown—especially if you're invited to appear on *The Tonight Show.*

ABOVE ALL, to cement in your mind the link between getting what you want and dignity, be sure that you understand the most fundamental misconception about dignity in our age of expanded "rights." Political-action groups love to babble about being treated with dignity, as though dignity were a right, but dignity is no more a right than love or friendship. The reality is that no one can be forced to treat you with dignity. Through a variety of applied pressures, someone might feel that it's in his best interest to *pretend* to treat you with dignity, but such false dignity breeds only hatred and resentment. So-called political correctness is a perfect example of this, so much so that it has evolved from resentment to comedy. When a concept is no longer taken seriously, where's the dignity?

Consider that not too long ago a Harvard history professor was censured for using the term *Indian* (as opposed to the politically correct *Native American*) in one of his courses—as though the word *Indian* makes a Native American less of a person than he is. A growing number of academic theorists have concluded that the First Amendment guarantee of free speech is subordinate to someone's "right" to not have his feelings hurt.

Worse, political-correctness advocates now claim that more than one million college students have been victims of "ethnic violence"—which includes insults! (Upon hearing this, I imme-

diately called my attorney and demanded that he file lawsuits against 7,248 people who have insulted me—in the last year, that is.) Some call it *political correctness*; I call it *insanity*. If violence now includes insults—insults that are defined as such by campus radicals of the 1960s who now control the centers of higher education in all Western countries—then all of my dictionaries are outdated. Violence is the use of physical force with an intent to do harm. Insults are a part of free speech, and subject to individual interpretation at that. Even Viktor Frankl, author of *Man's Search for Meaning* and a victim of three years in

Nazi concentration camps, admitted that intellectual honesty would compel him to grant Hitler the right to his views.

The road to a society where racism is minimal is not paved with coercion, but self-respect, and self-respect leads to dignity. Self-respect, as noted earlier, stems from personal virtuosity, thus dignity is derived from *within*. And from self-respect flows the respect of others—*as a natural consequence*.

In other words, civility has to do with how you treat *others;* dignity has to do with how you treat *yourself.* You do not have a right to be treated with dignity. You do, however, have a right to *possess* dignity. Demanding dignity from others is the ultimate self-delusion. If being treated with dignity is really important to you, the best way to bring

> You don't have a right to be treated with dignity. You do have a right to *possess* dignity.

that about is to act in dignified ways. And, happily, that is something over which you have complete control.

Also, make it a point never to use the shopworn excuse "everybody's doing it" to rationalize undignified actions. People who are busy achieving their goals aren't "doing it," whatever "it" may happen to be, for the pragmatic reason that undignified actions simply are not in their best interest. Remember, dignity is about *you,* not society. You can wear your hair purple, put a diamond-studded earring in your nose, and have a snake tattoo burned into your forehead, but no one has to hire or do business with you. Further, if you decide to go this route, I highly recommend that you not relocate to Singapore, where caning is a national pastime.

The fact is that no matter how decadent the world around you becomes, you always have the option of rising above the decadence and, as with civility, commanding the admiration and respect of others. Best of all, maintaining your dignity allows you to maintain self-respect, which is an all-important component of happiness and goal attainment.

Honesty is another quality that has given sway to relativism in many quarters. The Clintonization of America moved relativism up to a whole new level, as millions of people felt relieved to discover that lying was not a big deal. When Bill Clinton answered a grand jury question with the almost comedic, truth-twisting line "It depends upon what the meaning of the word *is* is," he was merely taking the art form of most politicians to its logical extreme. The fact is that Clinton was not so much a bad person as a bad product, the inevitable culmination of an inherently dishonest system and a society that had lost its moral footing. To parody an old preface, if Bill Clinton had not been born, the political system would have had to invent him. He was the ultimate politician—an embarrassment-proof, shame-proof, guilt-proof caricature of the perfect truth twister.

Bill Clinton's escape from the jaws of justice gave normal citizens with dirty hands a de facto presidential dispensation. Little wonder, then, that polls consistently showed that approximately two-thirds of Americans thought he should remain in office. With this as a backdrop, the fact that numerous other polls have found that roughly two-thirds of U.S. students cheat and don't see anything wrong with it is unlikely to change any time soon.

Call me a Pollyanna, but I think students really know better. What they are expressing in these polls is their *desire* to make cheating okay. It's a matter of self-delusion, of making true that which they love—and make no mistake about it, a majority of students love to cheat (or at least love the results of cheating). Since polls also tell us that the majority of adults regularly lie and, as with students, don't see anything wrong with it, the same self-delusion holds true. So, too, does the reality that they really know better. I agree with C. S. Lewis, who pointed out that "in our hearts we all know what's right." When two people get into an argument over a dishonest action, the argument is rarely about what is right and wrong. With few exceptions, arguments are about which party was in the wrong.

A broad definition of an honest person is *someone who acts with honorable intentions.* Acts of dishonesty, such as lying, stealing, cheating, and deceiving, tend to overlap. For example, a woman who was going to school at night once told me that she studied several hours a day while at work. My first thought was that she was deceiving her employer, but as I had time to reflect on the matter I realized that she also was implicitly lying to her boss (by omitting to tell him that she was studying at the company's expense), stealing from her company (taking money in the form of time without giving commensurate value in return), and cheating (in the same way that she was lying and stealing).

Which is why I like the broad definition of honesty. It keeps me on my toes, because it emphasizes *intent.* I can engage in endless debate with others about who was right and who was wrong in any given circumstance, but in my heart I know what my real intent was when I took an action. The ability to admit to yourself that your intent was not honorable in a given situation is a cathartic experience. It is also a sure sign of personal growth.

If it's true that people know in their hearts what's right and wrong, why do so many people consistently act dishonestly? The answer lies in that age-old nemesis, instant gratification, because lying can get one out of a lot of short-term discomfort. The other side of the lying coin, however, is that it almost always leads to *long-term* discomfort, which is the opposite of what we're after. The whole point of living rationally is to achieve happiness over the long term.

The Dishonesty Weapon of Choice

Criminal acts of dishonesty, such as robbery and embezzlement, are not part of most people's worlds, so when they speak of dishonesty they usually are referring to lying. What makes lying so insidious in nature is its many subtle forms. For example, the so-called *little white lie* is perhaps the most insidious of all lies because of its implied harmlessness. Additionally, what qualifies as "little" is subjective, so the little white lie has no clear boundaries. The danger, therefore, is that with the telling of each little white lie, one's boundaries tend to expand and, ultimately, the subconscious mind starts branding some pretty hefty lies as little white lies.

The *rationalization lie* is almost always based on self-delusion. Anyone with above-average intelligence can come up with a way to rationalize virtually any dishonest act. A rationalization lie is usually employed when one is convinced that he has been wronged, the implication being that two wrongs somehow make a right. Again, the problem is one of boundaries, because most people go through life feeling as though they are constantly being treated unjustly. If not curbed early on, rationalizations can become the catalyst for an anything-goes philosophy in all areas of a person's life.

Most people don't think of an *exaggeration lie* as a real lie, but in every sense of the word it is. From a practical standpoint, the exaggeration lie is the most likely kind of lie to be exposed. For this reason, I try to be especially vigilant about not overstating facts. As a writer, you learn (or should learn) early on that the power of understatement is enormous. Once you catch someone exaggerating, you can't help but to downsize all future comments from him. If you don't like the idea of people laughing at you behind your back, the best insurance policy against it is to not make laughable statements. It is decidedly in your best interest to go to extremes when it comes to understating your case.

The *hair-splitting lie* is based on technicalities, and is used by people who excel at being clever. To paraphrase economist-historian Thomas Sowell, the problem with being clever is that there is a tendency to try to continue to be clever long past the point where what one has to lose is much greater than what he has to gain. Nothing is more of a turnoff than attempts to be clever by being overly technical even when the facts are clearly against you.

The *omission lie* is the gray area of lying, because there is always the moral question of which information, and how much information, needs to be divulged at any given time. The best guideline is to ask yourself if the person to whom you are omitting a fact will be negatively impacted by your failure to disclose certain information to him. The omission lie gets right to the heart of honorable intentions. While it is the easiest kind of lie to conceal, once exposed it often brings more anger and distrust than any other kind of lie.

The *big lie* is reserved only for professional liars, most people not having the necessary genitalia even to attempt it. All of the types of lies heretofore mentioned might be likened to a scalpel, but the big lie is more like a sledgehammer—e.g., "I did not have sexual relations with that woman." Amateur liars can't get away with telling the big lie, so don't try it even if it's just for the experience of seeing what it feels like. When you tell the big lie, you can't be defensive when you get caught; you have to have the genetic makeup to be able to feign indignation and immediately go on the attack.

Dealing with the Devil

Honesty is not always as easy as many of us might think it should be. History is filled with stories about honest people who were reviled. More than likely you've experienced what it's like to act with honorable intentions, yet have people become angry with you for doing so. Often it's just a case of shooting the messenger, and when that happens your integrity is severely put to the test.

The Canadian-based company (hereafter referred to as "Vitahoax Corp.") that supplied my New Zealand company with products had been wildly successful during its first ten years in business, and boasted in all its literature that, among other things, it was debt-free. The mainstay of its product line was an herbal tonic (hereafter referred to as "Herbalsham") that was purported to improve people's overall health, from sleeping better to increasing energy. Millions of long-term users of the product swore by it with something of a religious zeal.

The product had become so well known and was so in demand that many Kiwis had been purchasing it from the United States, Canada, and other countries long before it was officially introduced into New Zealand. Thus, when the official opening was announced Down Under, there was a frenzy of excitement. Major distributors from North America made the long trip to New Zealand to promote the product. They talked endlessly about Vitahoax's altruistic efforts (always a bad sign) to "impact world health."

Above all, the legendary story about the life of Herbalsham's creator (hereafter referred to as "Dr. Hustle") was emphasized by both the company and its distributors. Recently deceased, Dr. Hustle had lived to the ripe old age of eighty-nine. Company literature explained that he had been a child prodigy, receiving a doctorate in agrobiology from the University of Vienna at the age of nineteen and a second doctorate, in biochemistry, a short time later. He was said to have held some twenty-eight patents, all of them related to his "love for humanity." An important part of the company's lore was that the formula for Herbalsham had come to Dr. Hustle in a dream.

Supposedly, Dr. Hustle had given his cure-all tonic away to friends and family for sixty years, only agreeing to sell it commercially when his son ("Lucifer") and a friend ("Pierre") convinced him that his creation could reach far more people worldwide if they could sell it commercially. So began a company that ultimately reached annual sales of about $250 million and won numerous industry awards. Not long after starting the company, Lucifer and Pierre took in a third partner ("Napoleon"), a supposed marketing expert whose job it was to make Herbalsham a household word.

Lucifer was said to have followed in his father's footsteps, having obtained a doctorate from Oxford University. His humanitarian nature was often emphasized in company literature. Pierre had no credentials, but was a personable, entrepreneurial type who had a passion for the company's mission to impact world health. Napoleon had even less credentials than Pierre, and came across as a used-car salesmen who had never quite made it.

After some rough early going in New Zealand, I managed to get things rolling. Sales continued to rise dramatically, and my company's results were praised by executives at the home office in Canada. In fact, at the company's ten-year anniversary celebration in Hawaii, I received a number of special accolades for making the company's franchise so successful, New Zealand by then being the number-one market in the world in sales per capita. The company, and certainly the New Zealand market, seemed to be headed into the stratosphere.

The euphoria lasted about two months, then came to a screeching halt when Vitahoax stunned the health-products industry with the announcement that it was bankrupt. As the shocking truth about the company began to unfold, worldwide hysteria set in with its distributors. With new pieces of bad news rolling in almost daily, the only solace seemed to be that things couldn't possibly get worse (always a bad assumption). Finally, the bomb: Not only had Dr. Hustle not received a doctorate in agrobiology at age nineteen from the University of Vienna or a second doctorate in biochemistry, he had earned no doctorate at all!

As you would have guessed, it also came out that Lucifer had not received a doctorate from Oxford. In fact, he had not graduated from Oxford; in fact, he had not attended Oxford; in fact, he had no degree of *any* kind from *any* university! Indeed, the apple never falls far from the tree.

Vitahoax Corp. was placed into a C36 proceeding in Canada,

which is roughly the equivalent of a Chapter 11 bankruptcy in the United States. Creditors, owed $15 million, were seething with anger, but they were not as angry as the two main partners, Lucifer and Pierre, were with each other. In a bitter struggle immediately following the company's collapse, Lucifer managed to wrest control from Pierre, who had been president and chief executive officer until things had started to unravel, by getting major distributors to back him.

Though Pierre, before relinquishing the reigns of power to Lucifer, had agreed in writing to make some financial concessions to partially compensate me for damages suffered as a result of Vitahoax's fraud and misrepresentation, I continued to demand that full reparations be made. Lucifer, however, now in full in control, had dropped his humanitarian façade and adopted an in-your-face attitude toward anyone who threatened to make waves. The hotter the fire got, the more Lucifer seemed to feel at home.

And, as the gruesome details continued to surface, the fire did get hot—more like a rerun of Hiroshima than the bonfire everyone had originally assumed it would be. Early on, it became clear to me that I had to send out a full-disclosure letter to all New Zealand and Australian distributors. Morally, it was the right thing to do; legally, it was an absolute necessity.

To my astonishment, however, when word leaked out that I was about to disclose the graphic details of the Vitahoax debacle to the folks Down Under, people from every direction went bonkers. I received angry calls, faxes, and letters from many major U.S. and Canadian distributors, all urging me to play ball with Lucifer. Other markets, Thailand and Indonesia in particular, talked to me at length about coming to my senses. It seemed that the one thing all parties had in common was that they desperately did not want anyone to do anything that might make Vitahoax's troubles better known to the general public. I was repeatedly reminded that Lucifer had the court's blessing to run the company under the auspices of the C36 proceeding, and that there still was time to gain his good graces if I would just work with him—i.e., go along with the scam.

I had always considered myself to be a reasonably sophisticated person, but I can honestly say that it had never occurred to me that anyone would actually try to repress the truth about Vitahoax, particularly when it was available to anyone who cared to examine the public records on the matter. So much for my sophistication. As slow as I was to come to grips with the reality of the situation, I finally figured out how it was possible for thousands of distributors worldwide to work in concert to repress the truth: They all had a vested economic interest in keeping the scam alive! In other words, they didn't need a well-thought-out conspiracy, because their short-term interests were concomitant.

Within a few months after the bankruptcy announcement, when the company was still $15 million in debt and had not paid a dime to its creditors, one distributor even went so far as to send out a notice proclaiming that Vitahoax was now completely out of debt. Many distributors stubbornly continued to refer to Lucifer's father as *Dr.* Hustle, defiantly demonstrating their hatred for truth in a way that only financial considerations can inspire. It seemed as though the whole world was involved in a massive cover-up.

Fortunately, though, it wasn't quite the whole world. Truth always has its advocates, and there was a small minority of distributors and corporate employees who fully supported me. In fact, it took on the aura of the American Civil War, with some families literally split by the Vitahoax scandal. People fanatically trying to repress the truth about Vitahoax often became angry with family members who had concluded that it was an immoral scam and wanted to distance themselves from it.

Working with one of New Zealand's top barristers, I constructed a full-disclosure letter and sent it to all New Zealand and Australian distributors. Then came the backlash. With the exception of the aforementioned small minority of ethical people, I was vilified and hammered from all directions. It was an eye-opening experience to witness many normally nice, rational people hysterically transforming themselves into hate machines as a result of having their incomes threatened by the possible exposure of truth.

I will not deny that the unexpected reaction to my circulating the truth hurt, but it was a hurt that didn't last long. It ended when a former Vitahoax vice president, who had been booted out by Lucifer in an effort to surround himself with loyalists, said to me, "If you really believe you did the right thing by fully disclosing the Vitahoax fraud, you shouldn't feel badly. In fact, you should feel ten-feet tall, because you had the integrity to do the right thing instead of going along with the majority who wanted to continue the fraud."

From that moment on, I never missed a moment's sleep over the matter. Under the most difficult circumstances imaginable, I had refused to compromise my integrity, and I felt genuinely good about my success in holding the line. The whole sordid affair reinforced in my mind my belief that the true test of honesty is what you do when either money or popularity is on the line, and in this case it was both. Those are defining moments when it comes to shaping the character of your soul.

WHERE CHILDREN ARE CONCERNED, the divergence of truth and popularity is particularly important to understand. If a child believes that honesty will always make him popular, he is destined to be disappointed. Popularity aside, however, children should be taught that honesty does pay, for two reasons. First, because it "feels right." It builds character and fuels personal growth. Second, because honesty does, indeed, pay dividends over the long term, and thinking long term, as I have stressed, is an important element in getting what you want in life.

None of us is honest 100 percent of the time, but that doesn't mean that we shouldn't *strive* to be honest. One of the best ways to do this is to constantly monitor your own words and actions, then have the courage to admit it to yourself when you have not acted with honorable intentions. Though it is true that there's no compromise between good and evil, a lapse in moral judgment that results in one dishonest act is certainly not as bad as repeating the same dishonest act over and over again. When it comes to honesty, late really is better than never.

Above all, never forget that you live in a world where you are surrounded by people who spend their lives trying to twist the truth to their own ends, so don't assume that it will be easy to be honest in every situation. An important key to guarding your integrity is to make it a point never to use the moral

> Guard your integrity. Don't use the moral standards of others as a guide.

standards of others as a guide. I've never met you, but I'd be willing to bet that you know right from wrong, so you don't need anyone else to make moral decisions for you. When people look to others to give them their opinion about whether or not a certain action would be honest, what they usually are after is a rationalization.

I've heard people say, in response to being caught in a dishonest act, "I had to do it. I had no choice." But they're wrong. You *always* have a choice. It may not be a good choice , but it *is* a choice. Honesty is *always* an option. You always have the

> Honesty is *always* an option.

choice of doing the right thing, no matter how unpopular it may be. As with undignified actions, never use the lame excuse that "everybody's doing it." The need to be praised by the majority is a sign of insecurity and immaturity. Having the courage to act alone is yet another sign of personal growth.

In this regard, one of the most widespread, dishonest acts bred by the everybody's-doing-it philosophy is computer-software theft. Most people don't try to rationalize their actions in this area; they just do it. After all, who needs a rationalization to steal from Bill Gates? Everybody knows that he made his billions by committing the unthinkable crime of giving consumers what they want.

Some years ago, however, I heard a unique rationalization for stealing software. It came from a person who had introduced himself to me as an avid reader of my books. What proved to be most interesting was that this individual had gone to great lengths to tell me how he was in total agreement with my moral beliefs. As the conversation unfolded, however, he happened to mention how many software programs he was using that he had not paid for, because friends had made "pirate" copies for him.

When I pointed out that it not only was illegal to obtain software without paying for it, but immoral as well, he said, "I don't look at it that way. In fact, I think I'm doing a software company a favor when I get a free copy of its software from someone." With morbid fascination, I asked, "How's that?" Whereupon he replied, "Because if I use the program and like it, I'll tell a lot of other people about it, which results in increased sales for the company." Yikes! Could this fellow possibly be Lucifer's distant cousin? It ranks right up there with "That depends upon what the meaning of is *is*." In reality, though, it was just another example of someone making true that which he loved, and this particular person obviously loved to steal software.

People can become pretty creative when it comes to rationalizing. Isn't robbing banks just a result of society's unfair distribution of wealth? Isn't infidelity just a way of better appreciating what you have at home? Isn't lying on your résumé just a way of helping a prospective employer make a decision to hire you because you know it would be in his best interest?

I should point out that just because someone does something dishonest does not mean that he is consistently dishonest. Even morally sound people sometimes cross the line. The problem is that, to one extent or another, we all tend to be selective, from whence comes the term "situational ethics." The woman I mentioned earlier, who regularly studied on company time, was a good example of this. My firsthand experience with her convinced me that, by and large, she had honorable intentions. Yet the temptation to get her homework done on company time was too great for her to resist, because her workload didn't keep her busy all day and, in addition, the company didn't closely monitor her work activities.

Another example of this was Donald and Janet, a salt-of-the-earth couple who once lived down the street from me. I would have thought nothing of giving them the key to my home, because everything about them indicated that they were honorable people. Yet, one day when I was at their house I happened to notice a huge collection of video tapes, and inquired what they were. "Movies," replied Donald.

"How many do you have?" I asked. In the most casual manner, he answered, "Over three hundred. Whenever I rent a movie, I record a copy for our collection." As he spoke, he pointed proudly to two video recorders sitting side by side on a table next to his television set. He then showed me how they were connected to one another, and how he could simply slip a rented video tape into one machine, click the "play" button, then click the "record" button on the other machine. After that, he could go about his business while his VCRs stole a free copy of the movie for him.

Your Moral Road Map

Because our senses have been so dulled over the past two decades by a seeming tidal wave of acceptable dishonesty, to achieve your goals requires a great deal of vigilance in this area. It's very easy to adopt an everybody's-doing-it attitude. I believe the surest way to prevent being ensnared by this flimsy excuse is to lay out your own moral roadmap as early as possible, though, as always, later is better than never.

This means that *you* have to decide what you believe in. *You* have to decide what you think is honest and what you think is dishonest. *You* have to decide where you want to draw the line on omissions. *You* have to decide if you want to be clever or if you want to be forthright to a fault. Remember, to get what you want in life, you need three things from people, and two of those things are trust and respect. And honesty to a fault is one of the best ways to achieve these. Whatever moral standards you choose, you need to have a clear idea of your values ahead of time, before being put to the test in a situation that tempts you to act dishonestly.

Also, remember that while what others think of your actions is important, you still have to consider the source of any criticism. A dishonest person will tend to criticize honesty, and, when that happens, having a predrawn moral road map will keep you from wavering from an act that you believe to be honest. The most important critic is you, and the most important question to ask yourself is: Did I act with honorable intentions? If so, stay your course; if not, make amends quickly and get back on course.

HUMILITY

One of the many wonderful things our hi-tech, global economy has brought about is the dismantling of corporate arrogance. Pure economics has forced legendarily arrogant companies like Xerox Corporation to come down off their high horses and bend over backwards to win back customers.

Arrogance usually stems from success-based delusion, whether it be an individual or corporation. The delusion—or, more properly, self-delusion—I am referring to is the absurd belief that one is indispensable, notwithstanding the fact that history repeatedly teaches us otherwise. Johnny Carson gave way to Jay Leno; Joe Montana gave way to Steve Young; Sears Roebuck gave way to Wal-Mart. You could spend all day adding to this list, yet barely make a dent in the number of well-known examples.

This was really brought home to me some years ago when I

was visiting Los Angeles and invited an old friend—an elderly gentleman who was a top television producer—to lunch. I asked him if he was currently working on any projects, to which he somberly replied, "It's as though I never existed." He went on to explain that a lot of his friends in the industry had died, and others had long ago retired or had their shows cancelled by the networks. Offers no longer found their way to his door.

My friend's simple comment has had a lasting effect on me. The surest way to set negative forces in motion is to start thinking that you're indispensable. If nothing else, death precludes arrogance, because sooner or later death eliminates everything about which a person has to be arrogant. But long before death, life also does a pretty good job of making a shambles of arrogance.

On the other hand, humility is a universally admired virtue. In fact, a simple but important truth worth remembering is: *People hate arrogance and love humility.* It goes without saying that you have a leg up in getting what you want if people love you rather than hate you. More so than any other virtue, it is all but impossible to fake humility, because what comes out of your mouth immediately places you

> Arrogance and ignorance go hand in hand.

in your proper slot on the arrogance-humility spectrum in people's minds. This includes how much you say, what you say, and how you say it.

Historian Will Durant, after seventy years of traveling the world, researching, and writing his classic eleven-volume history of civilization, summed up his life's work by concluding that "Nothing is often a good thing to do, and almost always a good thing to say." I would add that this is especially true when it comes to personal plans. Be humble; let people wonder and watch as your success unfolds. The more you talk about what you're going to accomplish, the more you invite the bad wishes of those who want to see you fail. Put another way, the more you talk about what you're going to accomplish, the more people there will be rooting against you. Who needs more obstacles? Success is tough enough to achieve when everyone is cheering for you.

Humility and silence, then, go hand in hand. The more truth you discover, the less inclined you are to speak. Speaking exposes one's ignorance, and the wise person knows that his own knowledge is miniscule compared to the infinite wisdom of our planet, let alone the universe. The corollary to this is that arrogance and ignorance have a tendency to be cerebral roommates.

There are not many things that can make a person look more foolish than pontificating on a subject that he knows little about, a phenomenon commonly referred to as "arrogance of the ignorant." Such childish behavior tends to set the eyes of one's listeners rolling skyward. The surest sign of wisdom is when a person knows enough to know what he does not know. I'm always impressed when someone answers a question with a comment such as, "In all honesty,

> Admitting you're wrong is a sign of personal growth.

I'm not well enough informed in that area to give a qualified opinion." As a result, when such a person *does* offer an opinion, I place a high value on it.

Likewise, clearly and promptly admitting you're wrong (when you are) is an almost magical way of gaining the respect and cooperation of others. I am fascinated by people who defend obvious mistakes with a ferocity that makes you think they believe they'll be placed in front of a firing squad if they are found to be wrong. Admitting you're wrong is actually a very easy proposition: Just do it.

EARLIER, I pointed out that trust and respect, as well as an enthusiastic and cooperative attitude, translate into added value in the marketplace. In reality, this is true of all virtues. When the virtues I've discussed in this chapter—civility, dignity, honesty, and humility—are evident in the same individual, can anyone doubt that such a person possesses enormous value? If you were an employer, do you think you might like to hire someone who was civil, dignified, honest, and humble to a fault?

Even in our age of modern technology, where specialized skills are at a premium, employers always have a place for someone who displays appealing virtues. Most skills can be taught, but there's not a lot of interest in the marketplace in teaching people how to be honest. It is therefore wise to have your virtues solidly in place before searching for the right job or approaching someone to become involved with you in a business relationship. Remember, personal growth does not follow achievement, it precedes it.

While the character of your soul doesn't need the approval of others, the fact that a virtuous person is usually easy to identify is a nice bonus. Such identification leads to trust and respect, which in turn lead to added value. And offering value to others is at the heart of getting what you want in life.

PEOPLE TAXES

*Principle #4: Avoid Those Who Drain
Your Personal Resources.*

> If you pick up a starving dog
> and make him prosperous,
> he will not bite you. This is
> the principal difference
> between a dog and a man.
>
> **MARK TWAIN**

While everyone understands that government taxes— federal, estate, gift, sales, and city, to name but a few— are a fact of life, the heavy burden of people taxes is often overlooked. By *people taxes*, I am referring to the personal resources (such as time, energy, creativity, health, and even wealth) you waste as a result of allowing the wrong kinds of people into your life. In effect, annoying, presumptuous, and abusive people of all kinds levy taxes upon those with whom they come in contact by draining away valuable personal resources.

101

When the drainage becomes extreme, it can result in a major barrier standing between you and the achievement of your goals.

Government taxes are a minor irritant compared to people taxes, as they are confined to a limited number of entities who demand only that you hand over a certain portion of your financial resources to them. People taxes are a much bigger problem, because they can be levied, to one extent or another, by virtually every person with whom you come in contact. Additionally, people can assess the same tax over and over again, which means, in extreme cases, that you can end up expending most of your daily efforts trying to satisfy your people taxes. Worst of all, people taxes can be levied against your spirit, and when you have to dig into your spirit to pay taxes, failure and pain are an inevitable result.

The good news is that, unlike government taxes, people taxes are voluntary. You have the choice of cutting off these insidious levies at any time. Nevertheless, most people meekly submit to paying heavy people taxes. Others accept only moderate taxes, while a small percentage of the earth's population opts for minimal people taxation. (Obviously, zero taxation is not possible in a world where one has no choice but to come in contact with other people on a regular basis.)

If you want to be among those who opt for moderate taxation, the rational way to go about it is to spend less time with people who impose heavy taxes and more time with those who impose small taxes. The latter would include individuals who only occasionally engage you in unnecessarily long conversations or irritate you now and then by arguing over a picky point. Some people are actually net producers rather than net taxers, and, as such, add net value to your life; i.e., the value they offer is greater than the amount of personal resources they drain from you. Obviously, to get what you want in life, these are the kinds of people with whom you want to be primarily involved. It's the heavy people taxers, those who assess major taxes against your finite personal resources, who are a serious threat to your well-being, and I can't think of a greater obstruction to getting what you want in life than allowing yourself to be abused by such people.

In addition to draining away obvious personal resources such as time, energy, and creativity, allowing the wrong people into your life can result in more subtle taxes. One is clearly expressed in the old adage that you are known by the company you keep. If those closest to you have questionable reputations, your efforts to build a respectable legacy will be for naught. I think most people assume that birds of a feather flock together, and make people judgments accordingly. Can an honest person really be good friends with a notoriously dishonest person? My benefit of the doubt doesn't stretch that far.

Even worse than being known by the company you keep is that you also tend to *become* like the company you keep. This is especially true of children, which is why responsible parents realize that close monitoring of friends is essential until a child reaches adulthood. Drugs lead to drugs; vulgarity leads to vulgarity; disrespect leads to disrespect. Children are very impressionable, and, as millions of parents have discovered—often too late—they are subjected to peer pressure almost daily.

Unfortunately, adults aren't immune to the problem of unconsciously mimicking friends and acquaintances. To some degree, this explains the phenomenon of spouses, in their later years, being so much alike. After thirty or forty years of marriage, how can one not help but adopt much of the thinking and mannerisms of his spouse?

Periodically, then, it's a good idea to step back and think about the people with whom you are spending your time. Where are their words and actions leading you? What thoughts are they influencing you to think? This kind of honest analysis can often lead to shocking revelations about oneself. Better to be shocked, however, than to blindly continue on with relationships that are transforming you into just the kind of person you never wanted to be.

Realistically speaking, you can't expect to achieve your goals without having to interact with, and receiving the help and/or cooperation of, other people. If you start a business, you need to deal with employees, suppliers, customers, regulatory agencies, and many others. If you work for someone else, you need to deal with bosses, coworkers, support staff, and anyone and everyone else directly or indirectly related to your job. Whether you play sports (even so-called individual sports), get married and raise a family, or travel the world, the reality is that people are an integral part of almost everything you do.

Even if you were to attempt to live a Thoreau-type life in the wilderness—a prospect that sounds rather boring to me—you would find the need to talk to people from time to time. Food and medical care are two obvious reasons why. The bottom line is that you need other people in order to get what you want in life. That being the

> Striving to be a self-reliant person will help you avoid bringing out the worst in others.

case, it makes sense to know as much about human beings as possible. Toward that end, the following is a review of some of the more important general realities of human nature.

Imperfection

We've heard since childhood that no one is perfect, and experience repeatedly confirms the truth in this adage. We learn this early on when we witness a coach swearing, a teacher punishing us for something we didn't do, or a parent not keeping his word. Notwithstanding, from time to time we tend to get so high on someone that we set ourselves up for disappointment. All too often, this disappointment stems from relying too much on others; the more we depend on someone, the more likely we are to bring his imperfection to the surface. Thus, striving to be a self-reliant person goes a long way toward helping you avoid bringing out the worst in people.

Selfishness

We've already been over this one: *All people are programmed at birth to do what they believe is in their best interest.* To the extent you expect people to act altruistically, you invite unnecessary problems into your life. You do not have a right to someone's love, friendship, or respect. All these, and more, must be earned. If you choose to act contrary to this principle, the result is likely to be frustration and disappointment. Remember, getting what you want in life is about creating value for others.

Unwillingness to Change

People rarely change their personalities or moral structures. Anyone can put on an act for a while, but ultimately the truth will become evident to those who know him. It's important to understand this reality, because we sometimes go along with a high people tax in the hopes that someone will change his ways. Unfortunately, it rarely happens. It is therefore wise to select business associates (to the extent possible), friends, and, above all, spouses on the basis of common values, such as kindness, patience, and self-discipline, to name but a few. Opposites may attract, but they tend to end up strangling each other; e.g., a marriage between people with conflicting ideologies—i.e., fundamental doctrine that guides their actions—is a perfect example of this kind of mismatch.

Situationally Ethical

Don't expect even the most ethical people to live up to your moral expectations of them at all times. All people, at one time or another, deviate from their moral beliefs; i.e., they are sometimes hypocritical. By now you know the lure: instant gratification. Situational ethics always require rationalizations, such as the person who robs banks because of his belief that wealth has been unfairly distributed. Thus, since people are imperfect, don't be shocked when an otherwise ethical, upstanding friend or acquaintance occasionally engages in situational ethics.

The practice of situational ethics is an unreasonable tax burden only when it becomes a way of life for someone. If I can never be certain of what a person's ethical stance is going to be from one occasion to another, I'm likely to spend way too much time debating him; worse, there is an ongoing danger that he might cause me harm whenever I make an assumption about how he's going to handle any given situation.

Easily Impressed by Money and Power

Sadly, most people are impressed by money and power—especially those who claim otherwise. Victor Hugo made an astute observation about this reality of human nature when he observed, "Prosperity supposes capacity. Win in the lottery and you are an able man." This reality constantly tests your character. It's also contagious, so you can easily pick it up from someone else.

The corollary to this trait is that when people think you're broke and powerless, they treat you with indifference, at best; more likely, however, you can count on outright disdain. Remember how the entire office staff ignored my assistant, Joanne, when she was perceived as a low-paid, airhead receptionist? After getting over the initial shock of her elevation to the top of the pecking order, it was interesting to observe how everyone began to defer to her judgment on matters of importance.

Susceptibility to the Three Fs

Most people, regardless of their basic personalities, have the potential to become very ugly when any of the three Fs—fame, fortune, and family—are at stake. Stories of people trampling one
another to get to the top of the entertainment ladder are legendary, and anyone with the slightest business experience has
witnessed the same kind of ugliness surface when large sums of
money are at stake.

Family, however, brings out the most neurotic, ugly behavior
of all. This is especially true of parents when they believe that
their children are being given a raw deal or are in some way being threatened. If you've had any experience coaching Little
League Baseball, or any other kind of youth sports, you know
what I'm talking about. A youth coach normally explains to team
parents at the start of the season that (1) winning is not important, and that fun and learning are his primary objectives, (2)
some children will play more than others, but everyone will play
the minimum amount of time required by league rules, and (3)
parents should set an example for their children when it comes
to good sportsmanship.

All parents assure the coach that they understand and agree
with everything he has told them, and most of them probably
mean it when they give such assurances. In fact, the parents are
friendly, gracious, and completely supportive of the coach—the
epitome of goodwill—until the first game of the season, that is,
at which time they begin acting like werewolves in the glow of a
full moon.

This neurotic pack of parent-wolves would be bad enough
under any circumstances, but heaven help the coach who has a
losing season (which is 95 percent determined by the luck of the
draft). When that happens, parents who were the most vocal in
agreeing that winning is unimportant shed their werewolf cos-
tumes and start acting more like prison rioters. If the coach plays
his lesser players as little as possible in an effort to turn things

around and try to please the win-crazed parents, parents of the children with minimal playing time become hysterical, even threatening the beleaguered coach with physical violence.

Tip: Regardless of how nice someone may have been to you in the past, when fame, fortune, or family are on the line, don't leave home without your best suit of armor.

SPECIFIC PEOPLE TAXES

Now that we've reviewed some basic aspects of human nature, let's look at some specific ways (i.e., specific people taxes) by which others can become obstacles between you and your goals. To the extent possible, it is wise to avoid unnecessary contact with tax collectors who impose, in significant amounts, any of the people taxes described in the remainder of this chapter. Keep in mind that these tax collectors can be spouses or partners, parents, children, friends, acquaintances (such as business associates and coworkers), or strangers. Obviously, it makes no sense to allow strangers or casual acquaintances to tax you too highly, given that family and friends usually will be all the tax burden you can afford to carry.

The Evilness Tax

I define an evil person as someone who enjoys causing pain, and goes about doing it in a premeditated manner. Anyone who has ever stared evil in the eye never forgets it. You experience a uniquely eerie feeling when talking to an evil person. It's an aura that makes you want to back away. Since I didn't create the universe, I can't tell you why some people are evil; I only know that evil people do exist. Fortunately, however, they are a small minority.

The danger with evil people is that they are almost all cunning. They wear personality disguises such as joviality, graciousness, and excessive kindness, and have a knack for gathering supporters. They come bearing gifts. They tempt you with flattery, and to the average person unaccustomed to meeting evil, the allure can be irresistible. Above all, they are master tellers of the big lie. When caught, they quickly take the offensive and try to shame you for questioning their truthfulness. They, in turn, are shameless.

There is a difference between an evil person and an immoral person. Evilness necessitates the absence of conscience, which is the surest way to know that someone with whom you are dealing is evil. All normal people, no matter how immoral they may be, have at least some semblance of a conscience. In the evil people

I have encountered, a lack of conscience was the most glaring trait overriding their cunning words and false niceties.

Truly evil behavior is rare, so there is a tendency for people to rationalize it away when they see it, which is exactly how they end up in places like Jonestown or Nazi concentration camps. While many Jews were unavoidably trapped during Hitler's evil reign, millions of others deluded themselves into believing that the situation wasn't as threatening as it appeared to be. As a result, they elected not to emigrate from Germany early on when they had the opportunity to do so. Understandably, it was difficult to comprehend the horrors that lay ahead.

While you undoubtedly will never be confronted with evilness to such an extreme, you will likely experience it in one form or another at some point during your lifetime. Be prepared, know in advance what to look for, and when evil does confront you, never be tempted to rationalize it away. Regardless of cost, move on quickly and absorb whatever losses may be necessary. No matter how great the temptation, you can count on the evilness tax being more than you can afford to pay.

The Dishonesty Tax

It's not difficult to spot dishonesty; the challenge is to do something about it. As with evilness, the tendency is to give people the benefit of the doubt, particularly if their dishonesty is not blatant. This includes individuals who exaggerate, omit material facts, tell little white lies, or regularly engage in situational ethics. All of these acts have come to seem relatively harmless in a world where dishonesty has become the accepted norm.

But dishonesty is not harmless. To the degree you allow a dishonest person access to your life, and, worse, allow him to overstay his welcome, unnecessary pain is bound to result. The main reason for this is that when you're involved with a dishonest person, you can never be certain that you're starting from a correct premise when making decisions. When is the person lying, and when is he telling the truth? It's too much to have to think about, too much extra work to have to fit into your already time-scarce schedule.

When someone misleads you—whether it be through exaggeration, omission, or in any other way—the result is likely to be harm, either for you or others. At a minimum, you may end up with egg on your face for making bad decisions based on falsehoods, which doesn't do a lot for your dignity. You could liken it to a game of moral Russian roulette: When you act on information supplied by a person who has previously demonstrated a disregard for truth, you never know what you're going to get. Remember, living a rational life calls for the conscious effort to make rational decisions, and it's hard to make rational decisions when your actions are based on false information.

> It's not difficult to spot dishonesty; the challenge is to do something about it.

The most shameful type of dishonest person is the prolific hypocrite. Virtually all people are hypocritical to one extent or another, but I'm talking here about extreme cases. The person who makes a pastime of hypocrisy—applying situational ethics on a regular basis—is able to do so because he has no moral obstacles in his path; i.e., because of his amorality, he is free to do just about anything that pleases him at any given moment.

Virtually all seriously dishonest people are hypocrites. Hypocrites are often easy to spot by their propensity for giving moral lectures, in many cases heavily seasoned with Biblical references. In other words, perverse as it may seem, dishonest people often try to make others believe they are morally inferior. If you should ever decide that insanity sounds like an appealing way to escape your troubles, an easy method for achieving such a state of mind is to try to get a dishonest person to admit he's dishonest.

Beware: Once an inherently dishonest person crosses the line and tries to convince you that it's *you* who is dishonest, grief and considerable drain on your time resources are inevitable results.

Do you really believe that spending inordinate amounts of time trying to convince a dishonest person that you're honest is an efficient way to get what you want in life? If you haven't had the good sense to have already invited such a person out of your life, his moral accusations are a sure signal that the time has come to do just that—clearly, firmly, and unequivocally.

The Anger Tax

One of the more fascinating experiences of my life with regard to observing human nature happened about twenty years ago. A friend had been trying to talk me into hosting a television series on self-development, and had put me in touch with a producer whom he thought would be just right for the project. I wasn't exactly new to the world of deal-making, so when I spoke to him on the phone I was completely conscious of all the deal-making rules—be polite, gracious, and humble; don't talk too much; don't oversell yourself; don't be patronizing; etc.

The producer and I talked for about fifteen minutes, and the conversation went exceedingly well. Before getting off the phone, he told me that he was very excited about the possibility of doing a show with me, and that he would get back to me in a few days to set up a face-to-face meeting. Later that day, my friend called, and I told him how well the conversation with his producer-friend contact had gone.

But a few days later my friend called again and said, "You're not going to believe this. I just got a letter from the producer I put you in touch with. Want me to read it?"

"Sure," I answered.

He then read, "I'm sorry about the Ringer affair. My chat with him on the phone was extremely unpleasant. I figured that if he was going to be so difficult to deal with in a first encounter, the next meeting could only be worse."

You might say I was a bit perplexed. Could it be that I had slipped into a trance and made an obscene remark about his mother? I would have searched harder for something I had done wrong, but since nothing like that had ever happened to me before, I suspected the problem wasn't on my side of the fence. After again assuring my friend that everything about the conversation had been extremely positive, he recalled that on a couple of other occasions he had been told that people had had similar experiences with this particular producer. He said he had not thought much about it before, but that he could now see a consistent pattern.

If you've ever had someone get mad at you for no apparent reason, this little anecdote probably had you shaking your head up and down. So the $64,000 question is, why do some people make a career out of getting mad at the drop of a careless sentence or misread facial expression? The answer lies in a simple, eight-letter word: *neurosis.* It is not my job, nor should it be yours, to try to understand what makes neurotics tick. This is serious medical stuff, so give yourself a break and let the medical professionals handle it. Why people are neurotic is one of those great mysteries of life. Just leave it at that.

It can, however, become a tax burden when someone with this kind of neurosis—a person who always seems to feel slighted or offended for no apparent reason—is consistently in your life. Those who have experienced this kind of relationship know that it ultimately deteriorates into a game of humoring and tiptoeing in an effort to avoid raising the other person's ire—which sounds like an awful lot of effort, not to mention an enormous waste of time resources. When someone gets angry at you because you may have said "boo" to him, best you start heading in the opposite direction—unless, of course, you're the curious type. But do remember that curiosity killed the cat.

The Nastiness Tax

Plain and simple, some people are just nasty. You probably don't have anyone like this in your life, because if you were motivated

113

enough to purchase this book, it's unlikely you would allow a nasty person to be in your face on a regular basis. Nevertheless, because of their numbers and the fact that they are spread over the earth in every imaginable kind of occupation, you have no choice but to come in contact with Nasties from time to time.

The nastiness tax is most commonly assessed in the world of retail establishments and service businesses—from coffee shops to airlines, from computer technicians to offices of all kinds. Lying in wait wherever you do business are members of that Homo sapiens subspecies called Nasties. A Nasty is the only humanoid whose growl can be mistaken for Godzilla. Unlike most other tax assessors, the reason for the Nasty's nastiness is not a great mystery. Scientists are pretty much in agreement that the source of every Nasty's problem is that he had his favorite rattle taken away from him prematurely during infancy.

This being the case, a sensible objective is to find ways to deal with Nasties that will cause you the least amount of unpleasantness. This is a problem for someone like me, because I tend to ask a lot of questions, and Nasties absolutely *hate* questions. If you want to witness a Nasty's best growl, try asking about a half-dozen questions during any two-minute time span. You will quickly come to find that it's an activity dangerous to your health.

Though they are everywhere to be found, Nasties do have their preferred occupations, with airline flight attendant and waiter being at the top of the list. One of the primary qualifications for either job is an "it can't be done" attitude, also known as a bureaucratic mind-set. While you occasionally will be confronted with a bureaucrat who is not nasty, it's a rarity.

Did you ever try to hand a flight attendant your tray prior to the designated tray-collection time? Never attempt this when the flight attendant is carrying a pot of hot coffee, as your lower body parts may not appreciate the result. Or how about committing a heinous act of aggression such as asking for a glass of water while the flight attendant is still serving meals?

*"Sorry, I can't take your tray right now, but here's
a little hot coffee to help you relax."*

I try to eliminate these kinds of flight-attendant hate crimes by eating before I get on a plane, or, if necessary, starving—which is preferable to being on the receiving end of a hot-coffee response. Compassion is in order here, because most flight attendants are nasty as a result of marching in too many picket lines. I feel especially sorry for flight attendants with large calluses on their hands, because it's a dead giveaway that they've had to carry union signs a disproportionate number of times.

WAITERS, more than any other kind of retail employee, are notorious for nastiness coupled with a bureaucratic mind-set. A memorable scene from the movie *Five Easy Pieces,* starring Jack Nicholson, highlighted these unpleasant characteristics in a comical way that made it easy for audiences to relate to. Nicholson, playing the character Robert Dupea, was sitting in a diner when a bored and scowling waitress walked up to his booth and asked to take his order.

He asked, among other things, for a side order of wheat toast, to which the waitress replied, "I'm sorry, we don't have any side orders of toast."

Irritated, Nicholson asked, "What do you mean, you don't make side orders of toast? You make sandwiches, don't you? . . . Okay, I'll make it as easy for you as I can. I'd like an omelet, plain, and a chicken salad sandwich on wheat toast—no mayonnaise, no butter, no lettuce—and a cup of coffee."

Increasing the intensity of her scowl, the waitress repeated the order, then asked, "Anything else?"

Nicholson responded, "Yeh, now all you have to do is hold the chicken, bring me the toast, give me a check for the chicken salad sandwich, and you haven't broken any rules."

The screenwriter's clever words in *Five Easy Pieces* certainly magnified the absurdity of the waitress's nasty, bureaucratic attitude. But with all due respect to Jack Nicholson, my experience with Nasties has convinced me that it's a bad idea to be confrontational when dealing with them. The thought of what the waiter or cook might put in my food to exact retribution for my insubordination is enough to steer me away from confrontations.

To the extent you can't avoid Nasties—which attempt should always be your first line of defense—I strongly suggest you learn the art of humoring them. For example, when a scowling, bureaucratic Post Office employee makes some absurd statement about why he can't accommodate a simple request; learn to bite your mental lip and say something like, "Gee, I didn't know that. Thanks for telling me; I'll sure keep it in mind from now on. Listen, you seem to be someone who knows how to get things accomplished [a preposterous comment that almost always works]. What would you suggest we do to make this happen? Do think it might work if we . . . ?" Then give him the solution in a way that makes it sound like it's *his* idea.

You can never totally remove Nasties from your life, so it will

*"Okay, hot lips, I'll make it as easy for you as I can.
I want a lox and bagel sandwich, no cream cheese. Stick the
lox up your nose, and bring me the bagel."*

pay big dividends if you can become adept at humoring. I am generally against humoring people, because it's a subtle form of dishonesty. In the case of Nasties, however, I consider it to be more a matter of self-defense. The only other solution I know of is to carry a concealed weapon, but is it really worth life in prison just to rid the world of one Nasty?

The Negativism Tax

No matter how positive your attitude, it's always a bad idea to be around negative people, particularly people who are negative about your aspirations or goals. Even if you try to ignore negativism in your midst, spoken words (not to mention facial expressions) are recorded by your subconscious mind. Just as positive images stimulate your body mechanisms to do whatever is necessary to convert those images into physical realities, so it is with negative images. This explains the phenomenon of the "self-fulfilling prophecy."

Regardless of any course of action you may choose, there will always be someone close at hand who is more than happy to tell you why you're making a mistake. If you allow too much of this kind of negativism to enter your brain, when difficulties arise it is quite natural to start wondering if your critics weren't right after all.

> Life offers plenty to be negative about, which is all the more reason to avoid negative people.

Aside from attacking your personal goals, some people are just negative about life in general. Life loves to beat you down, but you have no obligation to help it do so. To be sure, life offers plenty to be negative about, but that's all the more reason to avoid negative people. You need all the positive thoughts you can get in order to combat the never-ending stream of unpleasantness that invites itself into your life. In extreme cases, a negative thought can nudge a person from frustration to despair, and despair can rapidly become a terminal problem.

Further, remember that you have to deal with nasty people and bureaucrats throughout life, and they will gladly provide you with all the negativism you can handle. Virtually all nasty people and bureaucrats are negative, but not all negative people are nasty or bureaucratic. Which is precisely why negativism can sneak up on you before you realize the impact it's been having on your thoughts. Some of the nicest people I know are negative, which in some respects makes them potentially more dangerous than negative people who are nasty. When it comes to nastiness, you're usually on guard, but you tend to let your guard down when you're in the presence of nice people. This being the case, you should condition yourself to make tough decisions when it comes to not allowing even nice negative people to come into or stay in your life. Remember to ask yourself how many times you've achieved successful results when you were in a negative state of mind.

CRITICISM IS A SPECIFIC form of negativism. There's nothing wrong with constructive criticism, provided it comes from the right party. By *right party*, I'm talking about people whom you respect and who truly have your best interest at heart, in which case it would be more proper to refer to it as "constructive advice." Constructive advice from the right party can be worth a fortune to you over the long term; ill-intended criticism from the wrong party can do more to tear you down, damage your self-esteem, and prevent you from pursuing your dreams than just about anything else I can imagine.

As such, it is important to be selective about the people from whom you accept criticism. Do you respect the person handing out the criticism? Are his own hands clean with regard to the subject matter of his criticism? Does he have his own life in order? If the answers to any of these questions are negative, just thank the person for his "concern," then delete his comments from your mind.

This is one kind of tax that is often levied by those closest to you, particularly family members, so it can be an especially difficult tax to cope with. The friend or family member offering criticism may be well meaning, but his observations may still be incorrect. It gets even stickier when the criticism comes from a parent or child. (I'm talking here about adult children, as opposed to teenagers or young children. Young children are in no position to question parental wisdom, and teenagers, as we all know, generally tend to be confused about life and inclined toward self-delusion.)

> Be selective about the people from whom you accept criticism.

When a parent criticizes an adult child, in most cases the child would still do well to think long and hard about his parent's comments. If the child disagrees with the criticism, a little respect does wonders to help avoid a family war. As to a child criticizing a parent, respect demands that it be done seldom or never. Parents are entitled to their idiosyncrasies and shortcomings, and, in any event, because it's usually way too late to change long-established habits, they will almost never heed the criticism being offered.

Within reason, then, one should learn to live with familial criticism. But at the same time, one should be extremely careful about being too open to others who seemingly make a pastime out of criticizing friends and acquaintances. Writers learn this early on, because they are criticized regularly by total strangers, such as book reviewers and readers.

Ignoring professional critics isn't a matter of defiance; it's an act of survival. Writers, for example, would be suicidal to base their work on the opinions of a handful of critics. In this regard, two quotes have been enormously helpful to me over the years, preventing me from allowing my philosophy and writing style to be altered by critical comments. The first, which I read every day before sitting down to write, is from E. B. White: "The whole duty of a writer is to please and satisfy himself, and the true writer always plays to an audience of one." The second is from Ayn Rand: "Freedom comes from seeing the ignorance of your critics and discovering the emptiness of their virtue."

These two quotes apply to everyone, not just writers. It is both admirable and noble to believe in your work and your own code of ethics strongly enough to be able to ignore uninvited criticism. I'm sure you don't need me to remind you that to the degree you are successful, you *will* be criticized, because success breeds envy and jealousy. To paraphrase late-nineteenth century essayist Elbert Hubbard, the only way to escape criticism is to say and do nothing, which in turn guarantees that you will accomplish nothing.

Everyone has his favorite anecdote about famous people who were told they would never amount to anything. My vote goes to the critic who wrote of Fred Astaire early in his career: "Can't act. Can't sing. Balding. Can dance a little." It sounds more like a description of *me*—except I can't dance at all.

Negativism, regardless of the source, is a tax no one can afford.

The Rudeness Tax

I find that rude people are a heavy burden on my time and energy resources. I'm talking here about people who are guilty of everything from not returning phone calls to not calling to let you know that they're going to be late, or, in some cases, that they won't be able to make a scheduled appointment at all. There are also those individuals who are disrespectful in the way they talk to you, which is a discomfort you have no obligation to endure. Remember, you can't force someone to treat you with respect—i.e., it's not a "right"—but it *is* your right to decide whom to keep out of your life.

> You can't force someone to treat you with respect, but you *can* decide whom you want to keep out of your life.

Almost without fail, notoriously rude people use the excuse that they've been busy, which I personally find insulting. I can't imagine anyone busier than I am, yet I always find time to return phone calls and to let people know if I'm going to be late. That's why I don't have a lot of interest in listening to someone use so-called time problems as an excuse for rudeness. Dignity compels you not to let a person off the hook just because he claims he's been too busy to return your call. All he's really telling you is that you're not a high priority with him, and when it comes to business, in particular, that's a bad posture from which to operate. Rather than pursue a better opportunity with someone who repeatedly shows, through his actions, that I'm a low priority with him, I would much rather deal with someone who offers me less opportunity but demonstrates that he considers me to be a top priority.

Aside from the enormous waste of time and energy, an even better reason for making short shrift of rude people is that they can be extremely damaging to your self-esteem. Can there be anything more degrading and harmful to your self-perception than chasing after someone who is rude and disrespectful to you? Dignity demands that you expect the same politeness from others that you show to them. One-sided relationships are always a bad idea.

The Disloyalty Tax

Most of us remember Linda Tripp as a fifteen-minutes-of-fame person whose name came to be synonymous with disloyalty. What an incredible tax she levied on her one-time close friend, Monica Lewinsky. It was a high-profile reminder that even seemingly good friends with whom you have entrusted delicate information can sometimes turn on you, at an extreme aligning themselves with opposing forces. Good lesson to teach children: Friends have the potential—repeat, *potential*—to become enemies. You should therefore use discretion when it comes to sharing secrets, and even greater discretion when it comes to selecting the people with whom to share them.

At an early age, children learn that other children, usually acting under the influence of peer pressure, have a dismaying habit of switching friends abruptly and being cruel to ex-friends. One of the great challenges for parents is to help youngsters deal with this kind of betrayal without losing self-esteem or becoming overly distrustful toward all their peers.

Disloyalty, however, is not always a matter of betrayal. Sometimes it just involves people deserting you in your time of need. Everyone over the age of sixteen knows that the surest way to find out who your friends are is to fall on hard times. Which means, unfortunately, that you may go years before discovering that someone is not a loyal friend.

Notwithstanding all this, from the standpoint of living a rational life you should not allow turncoats or fair-weather friends to affect your self-esteem or outlook toward others. Like most things in life, moderation is called for when dealing with disloyalty, thus you should not permit it to make you paranoid about relationships. Just be sure to use caution when it comes to revealing too much about yourself, particularly when it involves your deepest secrets or highest aspirations.

The Free-Lunch Tax

In the movie *Cool Hand Luke,* Luke, played by Paul Newman, was a hopeless lawbreaker, a petty thief who entertained his fellow chain-gang members with his brashness and insubordination toward their guards. Because none of the other prisoners had the courage to stand up to the guards and risk incurring their wrath, they lived vicariously through Luke.

After numerous beatings and visits to solitary confinement as punishment for his smart-aleck antics, Luke finally appeared to have had enough. He became a model prisoner, toadying up to the guards and enthusiastically doing their bidding. His fellow prisoners began to revile him for his good behavior. Even though they themselves would never risk the punishment Luke endured, they felt he owed it to them to stand up to the guards.

As it turned out, Luke's conversion was just an act, a trick to lull the guards into relaxing. When the time was right, he stole one of their trucks, right before their eyes, and made another of his many escapes. Instantly, his turncoat, chain-gang pals once again revered him.

With pun intended, a good moral to this story might be to never allow anyone to chain himself to you. In this case, the chain I'm speaking of was a one-way emotional attachment that accrued only to the benefit of the other prisoners. Clearly, they believed in the free lunch, and came to expect Luke to provide it for them without having to give anything in return.

While this might seem like a prison mentality—something for nothing being a common mind-set of lawbreakers—it is, in fact, prevalent in all sectors of society. Some people are parasites by nature, feeling quite at home making demands on others without it ever occurring to them to give anything in return. At heart, parasites are both presumptuous and arrogant.

Like many authors, I've received my share of reader mail over the years, and I always appreciate those who take the time to let me know that they enjoy my work. Every now and then, however, I receive a free-lunch letter wherein the writer makes requests of me that would lead one to assume that we've been friends for many years. Sometimes it takes the form of a long list of questions, many of which would require hours of research on my part if I were to try to answer them. I have no explanation as to why someone would be so presumptuous, but I do know that it's not an uncommon trait.

The free-lunch tax can be huge, so it's wise to commit yourself to the mental toughness and discipline it takes to end it before it gets out of hand. Never allow the free-lunch assessor to intimidate you into thinking that it's your obligation to give him what he wants, no questions asked. People who expect something for nothing from you are morally in the wrong and therefore not worthy of your time.

> People who expect something for nothing from you are morally in the wrong and therefore not worthy of your time.

The greatest kind of free-lunch danger, and therefore the highest potential tax, is when the person who is all take and no give happens to be a friend. A relationship with such a friend can be a draining experience, and can take a long time to bring to an end. If you are presently in such a situation, the sooner you begin the process of ending the relationship, the better off both of you will be. Your free-lunch friend needs to grow up and confront the world on a value-for-value basis, and anything you can do to help steer him in that direction is a noble act on your part.

The Obligation Tax

The obligation tax is closely related to the free-lunch tax, but much more galling. This tax arises when someone unilaterally decides that you have an obligation to him. In business, this often takes the form of an abstract phenomenon commonly referred to as a "lost opportunity." I say abstract, because a lost opportunity is impossible to quantify, yet it is repeatedly used by obligation-oriented people.

My most unfavorite experience with the obligation tax occurred years ago when I was searching for a full-time sales and motivational trainer to work with my company's distributors. An acquaintance in Sydney had submitted a number of names to me for consideration, and I subsequently requested résumés from the ones in which I was most interested. I finally narrowed the list down to two people, one female and one male, and flew each of them to New Zealand for an interview.

I explained to the candidates that I did not want to make any permanent commitment until I had had the opportunity to see them in action, particularly given the bizarre reality in New Zealand that a job is an asset of the employee. I agreed to pay each a substantial fee for spending a week in New Zealand and conducting training sessions, and told them that I would evaluate their performances and let them know if I was interested in pursuing a more permanent relationship.

As it turned out, I decided against hiring either of these people, not because I wasn't impressed with their skills, but because I wasn't certain that the chemistry was right. I telephoned the female trainer first, explained my position, and told her that

I would like to keep in touch and possibly use her services in the future on a consulting basis. She was very cordial, and said that she looked forward to working with me again.

I then called the male trainer and told him pretty much the same thing, but his response was quite different. He went into a tirade about how he had sold his interest in a venture for the express purpose of going to work for my company, and how he was now left out in the cold by my not hiring him. After reminding him of the conditions I had originally outlined, I asked him how he could now be worse off than he was before his one-week tour of New Zealand.

In response, he railed on and on about his lost opportunity. He was now much worse off, he said, because he could have "had it made" had he stuck with the project he had been involved in for more than a year before I had contacted him. He never quite explained why he would walk away from such a lucrative opportunity in the first place. It was, of course, pure nonsense, but another vivid reminder of how some people will not hesitate to try to saddle even relative strangers with obligations created in their own minds.

The lost opportunity is the ultimate manufactured obligation, and the person who engages in it is likely to be telling his grandchildren thirty years down the road how he would have been fabulously wealthy had some thoughtless person not caused him to lose out on the opportunity of a lifetime. When someone gripes about your being the cause of a lost opportunity for him, I suggest that a justifiable response would be to turn and walk away.

The Irrationality/Ignorance Tax

A brilliant attorney once told me that he would rather deal with a smart, unethical attorney than with one who was irrational or ignorant. He said the problem was that there was no way to communicate his arguments to an irrational or ignorant person; i.e., no matter how logical and factual his points, they would have little impact on the other attorney because he would be unable to process them.

While irrationality may in part be due to genetics, it is a trait that tends to get worse as a person's personal circumstances deteriorate. A person may be born with the tendency to blame others for his problems (transference), but as his problems multiply he will tend to increase his efforts to look elsewhere for the source of his troubles. Which, of course, only causes more problems, and, as a result, the irrational individual becomes entrapped in a vicious cycle.

To a great extent, the same is true of ignorance. Genetics, of course, plays a major role here, but keep in mind that ignorance is not the same as stupidity. Stupidity stems from a lack of mental capacity, i.e., a person who is naturally slow thinking, or "dull." Ignorance stems from a lack of learning, i.e., a person who does not possess much knowledge. A search for truth is, in essence, a search for knowledge, so if an individual repeatedly fails in his search for truth, he will appear ignorant to knowledgeable people. The cause of an individual's ignorance may stem from a lack of education (not necessarily formal education) or simply from being taught, and accepting, too many falsehoods.

The reason I have grouped irrationality and ignorance together is that dealing with either of these conditions yields pretty much the same results. You can't reason with an irrational person, because he lacks sound reasoning powers; you can't reason with an ignorant person, because he lacks the knowledge necessary to understand what you're talking about. Thus, since you are unable to employ reason in either instance, whether a person is irrational or ignorant becomes a moot point.

There is, however, one significant difference between an irrational person and one who is ignorant. An ignorant person simply doesn't know the facts, but an irrational person's problem is that he is usually self-delusive, and self-delusion, as discussed in Chapter 1, blinds one from truth. A self-delusive person has a remarkable ability to ignore facts. He simply blocks out any information that contradicts his faulty belief structure and clings tenaciously to his erroneous beliefs.

This was true of my friend Jeremy, who employed self-delusion to rationalize his cult activities. He had the capacity to discuss most subjects—those that posed no danger to his cult beliefs—in impeccably rational terms, yet he would become almost maniacally irrational when it came to any kind of discussion that threatened the belief system that justified his cult activities. You may have found the same to be true of someone in your life. If so, when such a person switches to his irrational mode, you can bet he finds the subject matter deeply threatening. A dead giveaway to such an irrational state of mind is when a person repeatedly strays from the main point. When facts are closing in on an irrational individual, switching the focus of the conversation is a convenient way to escape being overwhelmed by truth.

In theory, an ignorant person with reasonable intelligence can be taught the truth, but is this really how you want to spend your life? Unless you're a professional teacher, you would have to place a very high value on someone to spend a significant amount of your limited time resources trying to educate him. When it comes to educating others, children are a full-time job for most people. You should therefore think long and hard before spending much time try-

> Focus your energy on cultivating relationships with rational, well-informed people.

ing to educate nonfamily members without compensation. A much more sensible idea is to focus your energy on cultivating relationships with rational, well-informed people.

The Debate Tax

The debate tax can be the most exhausting of all people taxes. By

the term *debate,* I am referring to the act of arguing, disputing, or contesting. An argumentative person is not only unpleasant to be around, he can consume large chunks of your time—time that could otherwise be used in constructive ways to increase your chances of getting what you want in life. An accomplished, incurable debater has the potential to frustrate and exhaust you to a degree only dreamed of by other kinds of people taxers. Whether or not you believe you are capable of outdebating such a person should never be the issue. The real issue is why in the world you would even care to try.

To be sure, an irrational person can also be a relentless debater. However, the added tax threat he poses should be a moot point, because his irrational behavior is enough reason of and by itself to keep him out of your life. Earlier, I suggested that if going insane sounded like an appealing way to escape your troubles, an easy way to accomplish it would be to try to get a dishonest person to admit that he's dishonest. But insanity is also easily attained by spending a substantial amount of your waking hours trying to debate an irrational person.

Because relationships with debaters have such a great potential for derailing your quest for a more pleasurable, less painful life, it's important to be able to recognize when you are in close proximity to a debater. To help in that end, I have summarized below "the ten dirty tricks of debating," the most commonly used tools of the debater's trade.

DIRTY TRICK #1: THE FALSE PREMISE

Basing one's arguments on a false premise is one of the oldest tricks of dirty debaters. It is a mainstay of most political debates, wherein politicians find they can slide the false premise by sitcom-damaged brains without much of a problem. Worse, supposedly opposing parties begin most of their debates with joint false premises, thus giving viewers all the more reason to assume that such premises are correct.

Doesn't every debate on social security begin with the premise that a social-security program is necessary? Doesn't every debate on health care begin with the premise that government should be involved in health care in one way or another? Doesn't every debate on regulating an industry begin with the premise that government has a right to regulate industry? In our modern age of big government, citizens have passively accepted such false premises with nary a whimper. Anyone who challenges these premises is labeled an extremist, and his point of view is ignored. In fact, almost any argument in favor of more individual freedom and less government control has long been considered a radical point of view.

In your day-to-day life, there is no end to the number and kinds of false premises with which you are confronted, though you have to be alert to recognize them. A hypothetical example would be when a person says to you, "We seem to have a problem, so I'd like to clear the air." If such a statement comes as a total surprise to you (e.g., the television producer who thought he and I had had an unpleasant conversation), you would be on solid footing to challenge the very premise of the statement with a response such as, "With all due respect, I didn't know we had a problem." Why enter into a potential debate (clearing the air) if the premise is inaccurate to begin with (i.e., if to your knowledge there is no problem)?

DIRTY TRICK #2:
USING THE DESIRED CONCLUSION AS A PREMISE

Using the desired conclusion as a premise is but a bold version of basing one's arguments on a false premise, sometimes referred to as an *a priori* argument. In other words, the clever debater merely restates his own conclusion as though it were a fact. Environmentalists are notorious for this, with global warming being their issue of choice in recent years. Most self-anointed global-warming experts begin with the premise that the earth is becoming dangerously warmer each year, though, to their credit, many of them have actually admitted that there is no conclusive proof that a long-term, global-warming trend is in fact occurring. Many of these so-called experts are the same people who not too long ago were warning of global cooling, a view that has now fallen into complete disfavor with the environmentalist crowd.

Of course, some people who employ this tactic do so unconsciously, with irrationality often playing no small part in their confusion. Whether or not someone uses this dirty trick intentionally, you should treat it as you would any other false premise and refuse to accept someone else's conclusion as a starting point for a debate.

DIRTY TRICK #3: PUTTING A SPIN ON A NEGATIVE

The term *spin*, which refers to the art of cleverly and smoothly twisting the truth, became popular in political discussions near the end of the twentieth century. It is now considered an essential tool for those who have dedicated their lives to the art of debating. The spin is, in fact, a dirty trick, and one that any reasonably intelligent individual can learn to employ. The objective is take a crystal-clear fact that negatively impacts the spinner, and twist it—i.e., "put a spin on it"—in such a way that it gives the illusion of being a positive.

Crafty politicians have become masters at utilizing the incredible power of the spin as a tool for achieving their ends. While most cases of spinning the truth tend to have an offensive nature, a spin can sometimes be lighthearted while still achieving the spinner's ends. Most of us can remember Ronald Reagan employing one of the most powerful yet good-natured spins of our time. In a debate with Democratic challenger Walter Mondale in the 1984 presidential campaign, Reagan responded to a Mondale reference to his age by saying, "I am not going to exploit for political purposes my opponent's youth and inexperience."

Most debaters who utilize the spin do not do so in such a good-natured fashion. Regardless, unless you're running for president, don't waste precious time debating spin artists.

DIRTY TRICK #4:

TAKING THE OFFENSIVE WHEN TRAPPED BY THE FACTS

Taking the offensive with an aggressive, all-out attack is a strategy often employed when the available facts appear to be undermining one's arguments. I once described for a questioner the aggressive nature of cult-member Jeremy through the following hypothetical scenario.

Suppose you're in your office, and Jeremy is in the office next to you. From your desk, you see someone walk into Jeremy's office for a scheduled meeting. After a few minutes, you hear a heated argument, then suddenly a gunshot. You run into Jeremy's office and find his visitor lying dead on the floor. Jeremy is standing over him with a gun in his hand.

Frantically, you shout at Jeremy, "You killed him!"

Jeremy feigns ignorance, and queries, "Killed who?"

You point to the body on the floor and exclaim, "Your visitor!"

Jeremy looks at the body, then looks up at you and retorts, "You're nuts. I didn't kill anybody."

You get tough with Jeremy, telling him to cut the dumb act and give you the gun. But, sensing that the facts are overwhelmingly against him, Jeremy lashes out at you. "This whole thing was contrived," he shouts. "I'm starting to think it was *you* who killed him. I'm going to call the police."

My example may have been a bit of an exaggeration, but not much. On more than one occasion when Jeremy was caught in the act of doing something unethical, I watched in awe as he turned the tables on the person who had confronted him and mounted a vicious offensive. The more overwhelming the facts against him, the more aggressive he became. He almost always succeeded in getting the other party to back off.

Don't be intimidated by an aggressive attitude, and don't accept loud, aggressive talk as a substitute for logic. When someone who is clearly in the wrong takes the offensive, more often than not it isn't because he's irrational. On the contrary, the attacker usually knows exactly what he's doing.

DIRTY TRICK #5: FEIGNING INDIGNATION

Speaking of Jeremy, an ex-cult member acquaintance of his once related a fascinating anecdote about how cult members were taught the art of debating. He and another low-level cult member had once been in the backseat of a car being driven by an individual who enjoyed a prominent place in the cult's hierarchy. A female cult member was in the front passenger's seat.

The car was speeding through a tunnel in which signs were posted warning drivers that it was against the law to cross over the center line to pass another car. Signs notwithstanding, no sooner had they entered the tunnel than the driver hit the gas, crossed over the center line, and passed the car in front of them. Within seconds, a police car, lights flashing and siren blaring, was right behind them.

When they exited the tunnel, the driver pulled to the side of the road, then turned to his cohorts and said, "Just follow my lead." He rolled down his window to speak with the officer, who chastised him for crossing over the center line. The policeman was about to start writing a ticket when the driver, to his surprise, lashed out, insisting that he didn't know what the officer was talking about.

Protesting with an angry air of indignation, the driver turned to his passengers and asked, "Did any of you see me pass a car in the tunnel?" Looking perplexed, they shook their heads from side to side and mumbled to each other that they saw nothing of the sort. The debate with the officer went on for a good ten minutes, with the driver becoming more indignant each step of the way.

Amazingly—and my acquaintance swears to this—the officer eventually backed down and apologized, convinced that he must have been hallucinating. When the cult members drove away—without a traffic ticket—they laughed uproariously. The officer probably never mentioned the incident to anyone for the same reason that people are often afraid to report flying saucer sightings.

Scary stuff—scary because of its power to alter reality. I have a simple rule when it comes to indignation: The louder and more vehement the protest, the less credence I give it. Make it a rule never to allow yourself to be intimidated by an overdose of indignation.

DIRTY TRICK #6: MAKING INTIMIDATING ACCUSATIONS

Making intimidating accusations is another trademark of political debaters, the objective being to put the other person on the defensive. Some popular accusations, both in and out of the political arena, include: "You're just selfish"; "You don't care about starving children"; and, the ultimate intimidating accusation, one which quickly brings most people to their apologetic knees, "You're a racist."

Incredulity also can be used to implicitly accuse and intimidate someone, as in, "Surely, you don't believe . . ." or "Everybody knows . . ." The idea is to make you think you're way off base if you don't agree with the dirty trickster who is trying to intimidate you. Don't buy it. Ignore all remarks that smell of intimidation, and relentlessly refocus on the issue being discussed—unless, of course, you're in a position to just walk away, which is always a superior resolution to the problem.

DIRTY TRICK #7: FOCUSING ON IRRELEVANT POINTS

Another effective debating trick when the facts are overwhelmingly against you is to change the subject. This is analogous to the magician's weapon of choice—distracting the audience from the sleight of hand that is really happening. Trial attorneys employ this art when they distract the jury's attention from any damning evidence against their clients by focusing on side issues and irrelevant topics.

Unfortunately, this dirty debating trick is also used by many people in everyday life, so be wary of anyone who demonstrates adeptness at changing the focus of a debate to irrelevant points for his benefit. Whenever I realize that someone is purposely avoiding the facts and trying to change the subject, I quickly try to put as much distance as possible between myself and that person.

DIRTY TRICK #8: USING INVALID ANALOGIES

I pride myself on having a logical mind, but from time to time I realize that I have inadvertently used an invalid analogy. Oversimplified, an invalid analogy is the equivalent of comparing apples to oranges. It's an easy mistake to make, because analogies take a lot of thought. Once I realize I've used an invalid analogy, whether I've caught it myself or someone else points it out to me, I mentally register the mistake, then move on.

Dirty-trick debaters, however, don't mistakenly use invalid analogies; they intentionally use them to mislead people. For example, a popular defense of an alcoholic is that alcoholism is a disease, just as muscular dystrophy is a disease. The analogy is, of course, invalid. Desire and self-discipline are sufficient tools to prevent or rid oneself of alcoholism, neither or which will help a person to prevent or cure muscular dystrophy. Another example would be an also-popular claim by many that everyone has a right to "reasonable" food, clothing, and shelter, just as they have a right to breathe. Not so. Breathing does not impinge on anyone else's rights, but for a person to be guaranteed food, clothing, and shelter, the rights of those who are forced to give it to him must be violated.

To the extent you find it necessary to be involved in a discussion with a debater who uses analogies, be sure to follow his words carefully and make certain that *a* matches up with *b* and *c* matches up with *d*. If you allow an invalid analogy to slip by uncontested, you're heading toward its natural consequence—an invalid conclusion.

135

DIRTY TRICK #9:
DEMANDING PROOF FOR SELF-EVIDENT FACTS

There is a whole school of thought revolving around the idea that everything is relative and therefore nothing can be proven. The philosophy of relativism teaches that the premises people use to make judgments vary according to their genetic makeup, backgrounds, and environments. This centuries-old philosophy was exploited and carried to its extreme in the decadent 1960s, to the point where hallucinating hippies argued that there was no such thing as right or wrong.

Using relativism as their guide, millions of kids ruined or lost their lives by basing their personal decisions on flawed premises. Feeling morally superior, they believed that they were searching for truth, but instead found only self-delusive nonsense. Given that the Beatles were at one time at the center of this tragic counterculture, I found it interesting to hear one of their members, an older and wiser George Harrison, say, in *The Beatles Anthology* documentary, "I went to Haight-Ashbury expecting [it] to be this brilliant place, and it was just full of horrible, spotty, drop-out kids on drugs. . . . It wasn't what I thought . . . all these groovy people . . . having spiritual awakenings and being artistic. It was . . . like the Bowery."

Three of the Beatles ultimately escaped relativism and joined the real world, but millions of their followers weren't so lucky. Yet relativism has remained a staple of the dirty debater's repertoire. An axiom is a self-evident truth that requires no proof, and rational, honest people do not require proof for self-evident truths. You do not have to prove that the sun comes up every day, but there was a time when it was necessary to prove that the earth revolved around the sun. You do not have to prove that not all human beings have the same skin color, but taking the position that people of differing skin colors have different mental and physical capabilities requires proof. You do not have to prove that no one lives forever in his present human form, but reincarnation, without proof, cannot be stated as a fact.

The relativist debater simply refuses to acknowledge axioms that undermine his arguments, instead demanding that such axioms be proven. As with invalid analogies, if you allow someone to base his argument on the contention that a self-evident truth cannot be proven, an invalid conclusion is also a forgone conclusion.

DIRTY TRICK #10:

USING INTELLECTUAL OR ESOTERIC WORDS

I used to enjoy watching the titanic debates between publisher-commentator William F. Buckley and economist John Kenneth Galbraith. It was the intellectual equivalent of watching Bill Goldberg and Hollywood Hogan clash in the ring. If you listened really carefully, you might even be able to understand a word here or there. Both men were masters at using intellectual and esoteric language to make intimidating accusations and deliver well-timed putdowns. To say the least, a lightweight would not have fared too well in such elite debating company.

In truth, however, both Buckley and Galbraith often used their high-brow language to obfuscate the facts. While such language makes for good entertainment, you should never allow someone to use it as a debating weapon. I am an advocate of Occam's Razor Principle (also known as the Principle of Parsimony), which states that the simplest route is generally the most correct. For our purposes, this means: Never multiply explanations or make them more complicated than necessary. An explanation should be as simple and direct as possible.

You wouldn't buy a product described by an advertiser in intellectual or esoteric terms, so why buy a dirty-trickster's argument that is presented in the same manner?

•   •   •

REGARDLESS WHICH DIRTY TRICK is employed, the bottom line is that you can't afford to waste time on people who turn every conversation into a debate. You must learn to rise above the fray, and the best way I know to do that is to tell yourself that whatever an impending debate is about, it's more important to the debater than it is to you. Is the resolution of a point of contention really all that important in the overall scheme of things? Very seldom. A debater becomes impotent if he has no one with

> A debater becomes impotent if he has no one with whom to debate.

whom to debate. Make it a point never to volunteer to reinstate his virility.

LOWERING YOUR PEOPLE TAXES

There are many other human traits that can be quite taxing—pettiness, laziness, and vulgarity, to name but a few—so lowering your people taxes can be a daunting task. However, keep in mind that there are no perfect human beings, so just because someone possesses one or more unappealing traits does not necessarily mean that he's going to be a high tax burden to you. The focus of this chapter has been on extreme cases, those people who have the personality tools to frustrate, anger, and exasperate you, as well as drain you of time, energy, and other finite personal resources.

Remember, unlike government taxes, people taxes are voluntary, so, in the final analysis, it's up to you to decide what the amount of your people taxes will be. You can live a rational life or you can pay excessive people taxes, but you can't do both; clearly, they are mutually exclusive. Assuming that you find living a rational life to be the more appealing alternative, I have listed below some recommendations that I believe will do wonders for keeping your people taxes to a minimum.

Don't delude yourself.

When it comes to evilness and dishonesty taxes, I caution against giving people the benefit of the doubt, and to a great extent that goes for all people taxes. It is human nature to want to believe the best about others, which is why we tend to make so many mistakes with regard to people. Learning to differentiate between speech and actions is very important to your well-being. As Emerson wryly suggested, "You shout so loudly I can barely hear your words."

> It's human nature to want to believe the best about others, which is why we tend to make so many mistakes with regard to people.

Again, the sad reality is that most people are impressed by money and power, and this human weakness continually tests your character. It also tests your judgment and vigilance when it comes to resisting people taxes. Seneca alluded to this when he warned, "A man who examines the saddle and bridle and not the animal itself when he is out to buy a horse is a fool; similarly, only an absolute fool values a man according to his clothes or his position, which after all are things we wear like clothing."

Don't delude yourself when you see clear indications of high people taxes. Save the benefit of the doubt for mild cases, but refuse to become involved with someone who displays extreme symptoms. An old adage warns us never to get in a lifeboat with a cannibal. Maybe it's my fear of being transformed into turtle soup that keeps me on my toes.

Never confuse good intentions with bad consequences.

A sad reality about people taxes is that individuals with good intentions can sometimes tax you as much or more than those who have bad intentions. This is when the going can get sticky, be-

"Could I interest you in my debating special, my little green friend?"

cause it often means making tough decisions about friends, spouses, and other family members. A spouse who continually berates you for pursuing your dreams is a classic example.

It still amazes me how many letters I have received over the years from people who have told me that they parted ways with a spouse or domestic partner after reading one of my books, almost always resulting in a better life. This used to make me feel uncomfortable, but after rechecking my premises I began to feel good about the fact that I had helped these people find happier, more fulfilling lives. Don't for a second think that I'm making light of divorce. If Churchill was right about war being hell, then divorce is hell times ten. But spending a lifetime with a person who makes every day of your life unpleasant is an even worse alternative.

Don't try to figure out why someone acts the way he does.

Yet another activity that can lead to insanity is trying to figure out why someone does what he does. Best you just classify a person's actions as one of those great mysteries of life and move on to better things rather than spending your time trying to understand his problem. Whenever I have an encounter with someone who is rude, negative, irrational, or just plain neurotic, I enter it into the passive-fascination compartment of my brain, then I forget about it.

Passive fascination with people's traits and actions is harmless, but if you allow your fascination to become active, you're opening the door to some potentially high people taxes. Again, this is a job for people in the psychiatric field who get paid to be actively fascinated. To the extent you choose to undertake such a job, it is you who will end up paying. Be humble enough to admit that you have no idea why people act the way they do, then move on to more important matters.

Don't try to change people.

At least one of the reasons why there is so much hate and war in the world is that so many people feel morally obliged to remake people in their own image. Even if such a lofty objective were moral (it's not), it would be impossible, which is why force is always used in the pursuit of such an objective. This ugly reality has been a fact of life since the beginning of recorded history, and, if anything, it is worse today than ever. Feeling compelled to change others is the height of arrogance.

Earlier in this chapter I listed as one of the realities of human nature the fact that people rarely change their basic personalities or moral structures, noting that we sometimes go along with a high people tax in the hopes that a person will change. In those rare instances in which significant change does occur, it almost always comes from personal revelation rather than through the efforts of someone else. Selecting the right kind of people to be in your life is a whole lot easier than letting the wrong people in, then trying to change them. And if a high taxer has managed to sneak into your life, it's a lot less expensive, not to mention

> Selecting the right kind of people to be in your life is much easier than letting the wrong people in, then trying to change them.

less painful, to evict him than it is to undertake the near impossible, time-consuming, and frustrating task of trying to change him.

Always control the situation.

When it comes to people taxes, it is important to be proactive rather than reactive. *You* should decide whom you want in your life, then take appropriate action if adjustments are necessary. Basically, you have only two options when it comes to ridding yourself of a people tax being levied by someone in your life.

The first option is to avoid the person as much as possible, which really is just a method of postponing the inevitable and prolonging your discomfort. The second option is to completely eliminate the person from your life, which is a permanent solution to the problem. It's almost always a good idea to confront a problem head on and get it over with. Elimination may be unpleasant in the short term, but, if properly handled, the long term benefits can last a lifetime. Just keep in mind that the problem is likely to remain in your life until *you* take action. To the extent you feel the need to ask the offending party for his opinion on how best to resolve what you perceive to be a problem with your relationship (meaning a problem in your life), you can count on losing control of the situation. If you see the other person as an obstacle to getting what you want in life, by what stretch of logic would you want to ask his opinion as to what to do about the obstacle?

. . .

ALWAYS REMEMBER how the king's wise men summed up all the wisdom in the world in one sentence. There is no free lunch when it comes to personal relationships any more than there is with financial matters. This is why the fewer favors you expect from people, the less likely you are to be disappointed. For all practical purposes, the supply of people who can add value to your life is unlimited. But if your desire is to be associated with decent people, you have to be prepared to pay a decent price. Along with good health and the search for truth, friendship and love should be high priorities in a well-rounded life. You should therefore be willing to add value to the lives of those people with whom you want to be involved.

As with everything, time is a limiting factor in finding people who can add value to your life. That being the case, it makes sense to waste as little time as possible on those individuals who offer only unpleasantness, which in turn will leave you with more time to find quality people who have the potential to be net producers rather than net taxers. Taxes lead to pain; added value leads to pleasure. Luckily, you have the power to choose between the two.

5

FREEDOM FROM

Principle #5: Rid Yourself of Major Encumbrances.

The greatest gift of God is
the freedom of will.

DANTE

Freedom goes hand in hand with getting what you want in life. There is no such thing as a happy slave. And if you're not free to pursue your dreams and achieve your goals, you are, metaphorically speaking, a slave. On the other hand, the more free you are, the better your chances of attaining long-term happiness.

> When people are free to pursue their own interests, value and wealth are created. There's no such thing as a happy slave.

People often feel imprisoned by such things as marriage, job, financial pressures, and just everyday stress, to name some of the more commonly expressed freedom thieves. Even the most seemingly innocent things can make you feel constrained to the point of frustration and despair, such as housework, household repairs, employees (if you're a business owner), school events, having to shave every day, too many houseguests, or simply too many commitments, to name but a few. In effect, the previous chapter was about achieving freedom from people who represent major obstacles (people taxes) to your getting what you want in life, which may even include friends and spouses. Striving to be free of obstacles in your path to success is the essence of rational living.

People talk endlessly about freedom, but rarely take the trouble to examine its roots. Freedom begins with a concept called *natural law*. The underlying premise of natural law is that every person owns his own life and therefore has the right to do whatever he desires with that life, so long as he does not forcibly interfere with the life of any other person. Many people, of course, do not agree with the underlying premise of natural law, particularly those who want to be free to curb the freedom of others. This is what most political action groups are about.

If, however, one agrees with the premise of natural law, he also is compelled to agree that no one has the authority to grant natural rights to anyone else, because human beings already possess all natural rights at birth. These natural rights include both personal and economic freedoms, and the only way they can be lost is if someone takes them away by force.

While virtually everyone claims to be in favor of freedom, there is much disagreement about what freedom means. One person's idea of freedom might mean his being able to do whatever he wants to do with his own life, while another person's idea of freedom might mean (and often is) his being able to do whatever he wants to do with other people's lives.

An all-too-true adage says that people get the government they deserve, and perhaps the most important reason this is so is because, notwithstanding the findings of the king's wise men, most people steadfastly refuse to let go of the free-lunch illusion. They want freedom, but they want it on their terms—which, above all, includes a warped notion of equality among people. Historians Will and Ariel Durant expressed the futility of trying to marry these two objectives by writing that ". . . [nature smiles] at the union of freedom and equality in our utopias. For freedom and equality are sworn and everlasting enemies, and when one prevails the other dies." Simply put, the message is: freedom or equality, choose one. The more free people are to pursue their goals, the more unequal their results. The more government and society try to intervene in human affairs in an effort to equalize results, the less freedom people have.

The greatest gift we can give to our children is to teach them that freedom is not about government- or community-enforced security and equality. On the contrary, freedom is about *insecurity* and *inequality*. The price of

> The price of freedom is self-responsibility.

freedom is self-responsibility, and self-responsibility means that no one has a right to anything other than what others are willing to give him, without authoritarian interference, in exchange for his products or services.

Don't be surprised, then, to find that when people espouse freedom, they most likely are referring to their freedom, not yours. What makes matters worse is that to achieve what they consider to be freedom for themselves may require a violation of your freedom. Thus, a great paradox of freedom is that in order to prevent someone with a differing notion of freedom from trampling on your freedom, freedom, to one extent or another, must be restricted. Which leads to the obvious question, whose freedom should be restricted, and to what extent, in order to "protect freedom"? This is a serious ideological question, and one that is beyond the scope of this book.

What is within the scope of this book is that even though every inhabitant of our planet is, to one extent or another, enslaved by government, people in so-called democratic societies are, within certain governmental limitations, relatively free to live their lives as they choose. Thus, while we can do very little about the areas of our lives controlled by government, the majority of things in our day-to-day lives by which we feel most enslaved are those that we do have the power to control. Some of the more important of these are discussed in the remainder of this chapter, and the good news is that gaining freedom in these areas is attainable by virtually any person who is determined not to settle for less.

FREEDOM FROM THE PAST

Who among us does not have unpleasant experiences in our past? Being bullied in school, getting cut from an athletic team, losing a sweetheart to someone else, the premature death of a parent, failing a licensing exam, an ugly divorce, or just being caught in a dishonest act are the kinds of things that stay with most people throughout life. Some things we're ashamed of, others we're angry about. But whatever our emotions about the past may be, they clog our brain's machinery and prevent us from moving forward with life in a positive, constructive way.

> The majority of things in our day-to-day lives by which we feel most enslaved are those that we do not have the power to control.

The inability to let go of the past is a self-imposed imprisonment, an imprisonment from which only you can free yourself. Being imprisoned by the past often involves dwelling on some great injustice one has suffered. The problem of injustice is discussed in detail in Chapter 7; suffice it to say here that you have two options when it comes to dealing with injustice. You can allow injustice to destroy the remainder of your life or you can use it as a motivating force to accomplish great things.

An important aspect of letting go of the past is to continually remind ourselves that no matter how much success we may have, no matter how wonderful our new marriage may be, no matter how much money we're now making, the past is etched in stone and can never be changed. So what rational reason can there be for allowing it to destroy the future as well? The more you intellectualize these self-evident truths, the more they will be adopted, through mental osmosis, by the emotional cells of your brain. This is similar to the concept of positive visualization—holding an image in your mind and thereby stimulating your body's mechanisms to do whatever is necessary to convert that image into its physical reality.

Another important intellectual aspect of letting go of the past is to refuse to use the word *but*. "I know it's wrong to think about the past, *but* I just can't stop" is a commonly heard type of response to the problem of letting go of the past. Or, "I know I can't do anything about it now, *but* if he hadn't been dishonest with me, I would be in a different position today." The variations are endless, but the essence is always the same. In each and every case, *but* is used as a crutch to hang on to the past.

> Refuse to use the word "but."

But is a word children should be encouraged to use as little as possible, because it is the starting point for the destructive practice of transference, which in turn is the gateway to failure. In this respect, it is very similar to the problems of smoking, drinking, and overeating. *But* is the most convenient escape hatch for the individual intent on avoiding personal responsibility. More often than not, when you eliminate the word *but*, you eliminate the excuse itself. Instead of relying on *but*, practice saying things such as, "I know it's wrong to think about the past, *so I'm going to stop*," and "I know I can't do anything about it now, *which is why I'm going to forget about it*." Again, the more you intellectualize such thoughts, the more deeply ingrained they will become in your subconscious.

Freedom from the past is essential to the successful practice of rational living. The conscious effort to make rational decisions is a difficult, if not impossible, task to perform if your mind is cluttered with negative thoughts about the past. The only contribution the past can make to your future is through the experience it has given you, and it is up to you to convert that experience into wisdom. The future lies on the other side of the prison door of the past, a door you possess the power to open and step through at any time.

FREEDOM FROM COMPULSION

Trying to be perfect is an unhealthy way to live one's life. I can attest to this, because I am, by nature, a compulsive person, a condition I've worked hard to moderate over the years. I say *moderate*, because leading an organized life and taking pride in one's work are noble objectives; perfection, however, is not. When people ask me to name the most important lessons life has taught me, at the top of the

> "Perfect" is the enemy of good.

list is the old adage that moderation is the best policy. While perfection brings stress to one's life, moderation brings balance.

What I've discovered through the course of my life is that "perfect is the enemy of good." When you have a project to get done, for example, perfection can be your enemy in two ways. First, an obsession with perfection can cause you to be late with the project, which in the minds of those who were expecting it on time can overshadow the quality of your work. In extreme cases, it can completely negate your work, which is what happened with the Microsoft Word reference guide I completed too late for it to be of use to anyone. There are few feelings worse than producing a superior product, then discovering that changing circumstances in the marketplace have destroyed the demand for it.

Second, since your mind's primary focus can be on only one thing at a time, to the degree you focus on perfection, you aren't

GETTING WHAT YOU WANT

able to focus on substance. In other words, perfection tends to focus on details (form) rather than the real objective (substance) of a project. As a result, perfection also tends to result in uncompleted projects. In absolute terms, of course, there is no such thing as perfection, so perfection is really an unobtainable goal—and an unobtainable goal is destined to result in frustration and stress.

The problem of focusing on form rather than substance is really part of a broader problem, that of not focusing on the most important priority of the moment. Compulsive people, as I know all too well, can be quite easily distracted from the task at hand. I've learned though experience that it's better to do a subpar job working on the right project than a great job working on the wrong project.

I believe that the reason people are late for appointments and events is that they compulsively get sidetracked working on projects that don't have to be done right now—in other words, things that have nothing to do with the objective of getting themselves out the door and on the way to their destinations. The bathroom mirror is not going to run away from home if you wait until you return from your appointment to clean it.

As always, the first step toward correcting the problem of getting sidetracked by low priority projects is to intellectualize it. I've learned to continually ask myself how important it is that I work on a certain project right now. Real freedom, however, lies in taking this question a step further and asking yourself, "Does the project have to be done at all?" Perhaps nothing has done more to free me than developing the habit of answering this question with brutal honesty. A task may be interesting, fascinating, or even helpful, but whether or not it is really necessary is a much more important consideration.

All of which points to the conclusion that the quickest way to finish a project is to not do it at all. I constantly try to remind myself not to become a slave to noncrucial matters. If you're gainfully employed, you know all too well that there are not

enough hours in a day to do
everything that is asked of you
and everything that you would
like to do. It therefore makes

> Don't become a slave to
> non-crucial matters.

sense to spend as little time as possible on projects that have little or nothing to do with furthering your efforts to get what you
want in life.

CLOSELY RELATED TO the problem of working on noncrucial
matters is the problem of saving too many documents and files.
This common ailment is caused by the subconscious mind's annoying habit of asking, "What if?" This file contains documents
that I haven't looked at in five years, but I don't feel comfortable
throwing it away. Why? Because, *what if* I need to refer to some of
the documents at a later date?

The what-if compulsion is part of a broader compulsion
known as the CYA (cover your anatomy) philosophy. This is a philosophy that places an inordinately high priority on trying to
make certain that you will never be blamed for anything and will
always be able to quickly find the precise item or answer you
need to solve any problem in your life. Living a CYA life is devas-
tating to one's creativity and capacity for enjoyment, and definitely a barrier to achieving one's goals.

In addition, it tends to result in a person's garage being filled
with cartons of twenty-year-old files, a suffocating enslavement
to which I can attest. I didn't begin making a serious dent in getting rid of old junk files until I started asking myself, "What are
the consequences of not having this file or document if I should
need it down the road?" In all but a few cases, the answer was
that not only were the odds overwhelmingly against my ever
needing it, but clearly my world would not come to an end if I did
need it and couldn't put my hands on it.

Another example of a CYA life is to be found in the compul-

sion to fill out and mail every warranty card. Have you ever pur-
chased an extensive computer setup with a variety of software
and add-ons? After the technician finishes setting you up, he
leaves behind empty boxes and
a stack of warranty cards. Filling
out warranty cards gives me
chest pains. Which would be
bad enough in itself, but what
makes it all the more painful is that you know you probably will
never need to use the warranties. The few times I have called
upon a manufacturer to make good on a warranty, either the warranty had already expired or the repairs could be done without
the warranty card being on file.

> Focus on what *is*,
> not what *if*.

Basing your life on "what if's" is a compulsion that can enslave you till the day you die. *What if* is not real; it's a hypothetical. Better to spend your limited amount of time-and-energy
resources on what *is*.

Obviously, there is no end to the number of things about
which a person can be compulsive, including smoking, drinking,
and overeating. But in all cases I believe the remedy is the same.
It begins with repetitive intellectualization—which is really just
a search for truth—which in turn stimulates the emotional cells
of your brain to take corrective action.

FREEDOM FROM THE NEED TO
PROVE YOU'RE RIGHT

Many of us suffer from the need to prove we're right, a need that
gets in the way of working on things that can move us closer to
achieving our goals. A classic example of this is a painful experience I endured a few years back. My wife had noticed some damage to the roof of our house, and made an appointment with a
roofing company (hereafter referred to as "Stick-it-to-'em Roofing") to come out and fix it. The morning of the appointment, I

happened to be at home. More than an hour after the scheduled time, the roofers still had not arrived, and I was on the verge of being late for a meeting.

Just as I was preparing to leave the house, the doorbell rang. Sure enough, standing before me were two men from Stick-it-to-'em Roofing. They could barely speak English, and what words they did manage to utter were camouflaged by a thick Spanish accent. Realizing they would probably have trouble understanding me, I spoke slowly and clearly, explaining that I was about to leave the house. Then, as an afterthought, I said, "Look, if you don't need me here, you can go up and fix the roof, but I have to leave in two minutes. The two men nodded pleasantly, and uttered some more "Spanglish" that indicated they would go ahead and do the repairs.

A couple of minutes later, I got into my car, started the engine, and began to back out of the garage. Suddenly, I heard a loud commotion and something hitting the back of my car. For a second, I thought it might be an earthquake.

I jumped out and went around to the rear of the car to see what had happened. To my surprise, a long, heavy ladder was lying on the right rear of my car. Then, from the roof, I heard now familiar voices rapidly talking to me in apologetic Spanglish. I was quite disturbed, and angrily asked the men why they had put their ladder behind my car, especially since I had just told them I was leaving. It goes without saying that I could not understand their response, but they continued to address me in apologetic tones.

As they shimmied their way to the ground, I examined the right side and trunk of my car, and was dismayed to see that the damage from the ladder was extensive. I told the two workers that Stick-it-to-'em Roofing was going to have to pay for the damages, in response to which they kept repeating, with apologetic gestures, "Si! Si!" I assumed that Stick-it-to-'em Roofing would be embarrassed over their employees' ignorant placement of the ladder, so the main focus of my thoughts was on wondering how

"You imbeciles! Stick-it-to'em Roofing is going to have to pay for this."

long I would have to be without my car while the necessary repairs were being made.

Over the next week, I made a dozen phone calls to Stick-it-to-
'em Roofing, continually being referred from one person to another until I was finally assured that I was talking to the person
who handled the company's claims (hereafter referred to as "Mr.
Cute"). Mr. Cute claimed to know nothing about the accident
but said that he would check it out and get back to me in a few
days. A week passed without a call. Over the next two weeks, I left
a half dozen more messages for him without receiving a single
return call.

About the time I was on the verge of losing patience with being ignored, Mr. Cute finally picked up the receiver on one of my calls. He told me that Stick-it-to-'em's insurance company handled all claims, and that I should have my insurance company call them. I protested, pointing out that an insurance company was nothing more than a front for legalized theft (as in, "Pay your premiums on time, but don't expect us to pay your claims without a protracted legal battle"). Realizing that my insurance company would have little interest in filing a lawsuit against his company for $2,000, I said, "Look, just pay for the damage you did to my car, and if you want to collect from your insurance company, that's your business." Mr. Cute said he would have to check it out with Mr. Stickitoem himself, and would get back to me.

Weeks later, when I finally succeeded in getting Mr. Cute on the phone again, he explained that there was nothing more he could do about the matter, because the workers who had come to my house were now supposedly claiming they had told me that they were going to put the ladder behind my car, and that it was therefore *my* fault. I was livid. Quite obviously, the workers' new story was contrived by the company, and they would of course be willing to swear to whatever the company instructed them to say.

"First," I said, "these guys can't speak English, so even if they had told me they were going to put their ladder behind my garage door, I could not have understood them. Second, nobody in his right mind would tell you that he's going to put a ladder directly behind your garage door when he has the entire house to use. The moment your workers made the stupid mistake of putting their ladder behind my garage door, Stick-it-to-'em Roofing became liable, regardless of what your workers claim they told me. Third, I don't for a second believe they actually told you that. What I do believe is that *you* told them to say it. Fourth, why didn't you tell me all this months ago when I first spoke to you, instead of implying that fault was not even an issue?" I went on to tell Mr. Cute that unless Stick-it-to-'em Roofing paid for the damage to my car within a week, I would file suit in small claims court.

Needless to say, no one from the company called me again, let alone paid for the damage, so, as promised, I filed suit in small claims court. Over the next several months, I stood in lines at the court house, burned the midnight oil filling out legal forms, visited car-repair shops and secured estimates, did a mountain of research, and spent obscene amounts of time standing over a copying machine, making copies, sorting documents, and setting up files for the case. To a fly on the wall, it must have appeared as though I were preparing for a murder trial.

What had in fact happened was that I had developed an obsession to prove I was right, which means I had also lost my capacity to make conscious, rational decisions. As Stick-it-to-'em Roofing injected one obstacle after another into this penny-ante case in an effort to stall, I finally started coming to my senses. I realized that I had allowed my emotions to entrap me in a no-win situation. There was no doubt in my mind that the court would order Stick-it-to-'em Roofing to pay me $2,000 in damages, but that wouldn't even make a dent in the income I had lost as a result of my vigorous pursuit of justice. Worse, the stress and anxiety I had suffered from all this was impossible to quantify.

When the court date finally arrived, I showed up at 8:00 A.M., eager to bring the matter to a conclusion. There is nothing quite as stimulating as sitting on a hard bench and listening to small claims cases—Mr. Smith's dog ruined my rose garden; Mrs. O'Neil's son drove his car over my lawn; Mr. Wilson wrote our store a personal check for his groceries, ate the evidence, then claimed the food was spoiled and stopped payment on his check; etc., etc., etc. As the hours droned on, I didn't know whether to yawn, laugh, or cry.

Finally, the moment of truth—my case was called. A shyster-looking attorney (hereafter referred to as "Legalsleaze") in a vomit-colored, polyester suit came forward on behalf of Stick-it-to-'em Roofing. As I stood dutifully next to him before the presiding judge, the first thing that crossed my mind was that Stick-it-to-'em Roofing had probably bartered his fees. Why else would Legalsleaze use the same stuff on his hair that the company used for tarring roofs?

The judge then asked Legalsleaze to state his position on the case. What came out of his mouth was yet another reminder of how the legal system works—which is to say that it doesn't. He said that since his client believed I was at fault, it wanted to sue *me* to recover its legal fees, and that would require "full discovery," meaning depositions, interrogatories, etc. All this would require at least a year to accomplish, perhaps two years if enough clever stalling tactics were employed. Legalsleaze asked that the case therefore be moved to Superior Court for a full-blown trial. Still reeling, I listened as the judge said that he had no choice but to grant Legalsleaze his request.

As I left the courthouse, I started laughing at myself out loud. The next day, I dropped the suit, licked my wounds, and got back to working on constructive matters. It was a painful, time-wasting experience that served as a grim reminder of just how irrational it is to allow yourself to become obsessed with proving you're right.

As I said in offering caution about becoming involved with a debater, the best way I know to become free of the self-imposed obligation to prove you're right is to tell yourself that whatever the argument or disagreement is about, it's more important to the other person than it is to you. Is the resolution of a point

> If you know you're right, you have nothing to gain by telling someone he's wrong.

of contention really all that important in the overall scheme of things? Very seldom. Two thousand dollars may have looked like a significant sum of money when I began my Stick-it-to-'em legal journey, but by the time I came to my senses and threw in the towel, it was a pittance compared to what I had lost in time and emotional well-being.

Fortunately, the Stick-it-to-'em Roofing episode was an exception for me, albeit an expensive one. Every day of my life I hear people say many things with which I disagree, but I rarely argue with them. In fact, the more confident I am that I'm right, the less inclined I am to challenge an incorrect statement. I feel that if I know I'm right, I have nothing to gain by telling someone he's wrong. It could cause hard feelings, or, worse, lead to a debate, and I gave up on debating a long time ago.

One exception to this is when it's an individual who is involved in a project that I'm working on, and his incorrect statement is material to the success of the project. In such a case, there obviously is a necessity for the other person to understand the facts. Another exception is when I'm *not* 100 percent certain that I'm right, in which case it is, of course, prudent to discuss the matter with the other person.

Nothing could be better for you than an honest search for truth; nothing could be worse for you than a stubborn obsession with proving you're right.

FREEDOM FROM "WHY?"

Supersuccessful people seem to have at least one thing in common: They are not deep thinkers. For example, some years ago, when Steven Spielberg was a guest on *Larry King Live,* King asked him if he ever thought about what it was that allowed him to come up with one creative project after another. With a perplexed expression on his face, he said, "Gee, I've never really given it any thought. I think I'd be afraid that if I thought about it too much, I might lose whatever it is that makes it possible for me to do it."

Another example was in one of Mark McGwire's many interviews after breaking Roger Maris's home-run record when he was asked how he had managed to handle the pressure. Replied McGwire, "I don't know how I did it. I don't know if I want to know how I did it."

Some people might tend to view my lack-of-deep-thinking observation as insulting, but it all depends on their premise. If someone believes that deep thinking is inherently good, then I suppose a lack of deep thinking could be construed as bad. But if deep thinking is not viewed as either good or bad, it becomes just a matter of fascination; i.e., why do some people think deeply and others don't? Further, what are the ramifications of being a deep thinker, and what are the ramifications of not being a deep thinker?

When Frank Sinatra died, newspapers around the world covered his life and death in minute detail. Of particular interest to me was an article that listed some of "Sinatra's Rules." One of the more fascinating things he was purported to have believed in was that "people shouldn't think too much." Based on this, if Sinatra and, say, a legendary writer/philosopher like Fyodor Dostoevsky had each been asked to look at a rock, then relate their thoughts about it, their answers undoubtedly would have been quite different. From what we know about each of these famous men, it would be reasonable to assume that Sinatra might have said something like, "I see a rock. What's the big deal?" Dostoyevsky, on the other hand, might have said, "I see a rock, but I wonder what is inside the rock and what is it made of? Why does the rock exist? What is its true purpose?"

Thus, Sinatra would have dispensed with the rock question in seconds, while Dostoyevsky probably would have added it to a storehouse of similar questions that consumed his mind, to be thought about periodically through the rest of his life. Which one is better off depends upon your premise. If fame, fortune, and fun are your objectives, then best you heed Sinatra's words. If intellectually dismantling everything that crosses your path gives you a great deal of pleasure, then Dostoevsky is your man.

As always, I lean toward moderation. If you're serious about searching for truth, you're bound to do a great deal of deep thinking. Deep thinking, however, becomes a problem when carried to an extreme or when it evolves into what I call the *why* syndrome. Unless you're working toward a master's degree in rocks, is it really important to know *why* the rock exists? From a utilitarian point of view, the fact that the rock exists and that you do or do not have use for it is sufficient information. The simplicity of such an observation allows the utilitarian to move quickly on to more important matters in his life, which is much more conducive to success.

My guess is that *why* thinkers tend to have more stress, higher blood pressure, and far less productivity than non-*why* thinkers. To the extent you suffer from any of these maladies, you may want to take a more vigorous approach to freeing yourself from the *why's* in your life. The worst thing about being a *why* thinker is that when you exit this life, you may not know a whole lot more about it than someone who has never thought to ask *why* about anything. Actually, there's one thing even worse. What if you do know more about life than people who never ask *why*, but in the end you discover that it doesn't matter?

For example, if spirituality is high on your list when it comes to a search for truth, consider the possibility that it may very well be that "connecting" with a Higher Source may be more difficult for the individual whose mind is cluttered by a million and one *why's*. Viktor Frankl, in his book *Man's Search for Meaning*, addresses this possibility by speculating that a mentally retarded person, because his mind is uncluttered, may have a superior capacity to be spiritual.

I am not in any way suggesting that you should curb your search for truth; searching for truth is an essential ingredient for success. What I am suggesting, however, is that you should be selective when it comes to asking the question *why*.

Give the major television networks credit for one thing, they understand that sexual decadence and racial hatred sell. By featuring these sick themes ad nauseam on most daytime talk shows, they succeed in titillating their audiences into wanting still more.

One of the more absurd offerings on this tired subject was aired in the early 1990s by Phil Donahue, former king of talk-show decadence. On this particular show, Donahue's guests included three young black activists and a black Princeton University professor with a 1960s activist background. With Donahue demonically pouring verbal gasoline on the racial fires, the black activists let the whites in the audience know, in no uncertain terms, that they considered them to be the enemy.

One groveling young white man in the audience explained that he was a member of an all-white acting company, and that his group was in the process of producing a show about civil rights. With a whimpering plea in his voice, he asked the black activists, "Am I the enemy, too?" To which one of the activists responded inexplicably, "Do you love America?" The white actor meekly answered in the affirmative. The activist, smelling blood, admonished him with, "Well, you got problems." Blacks in the audience hooted and howled their approval; whites in the audience booed.

Another activist went into a long tirade about whites owing him a debt for enslaving his ancestors, defiantly warning, "And we're here to collect it!" Blacks in the audience hooted and howled their approval; whites in the audience booed.

Moving in for the kill, rabble-rousing Donahue read some lyrics from a rap "song" recorded by a character named Ice Cube, which said, in part:

> Get rid of that devil, real simple.
> Put a bullet in his temple.

*'Cause you can't get a nigga for life crew,
With a white Jew telling you what to do.*

Blacks in the audience hooted and howled their approval; whites in the audience booed.

During an unintelligible diatribe, one of the activists suddenly yelled out, again for no explicable reason, "I'm an African! I'm in exile!" Nice rhetoric, but few blacks are seriously interested in leaving the United States, where most would agree that they are far better off than blacks in any African country. Walter Williams, a black economics professor at George Mason University and a champion of self-responsibility, put it succinctly when he asked, "What has Afrocentrism done for Africa?"

Most black Americans realize that white folks are never going to open their arms to blacks who cling to so-called Afrocentrism. The more some blacks choose to group themselves as "African," the more the fires of racism will be stoked. The biggest obstacles to diffusing this in-your-face attitude are the black hatemongers who ludicrously insist that every black who makes it in America has sold out. Self-anointed black leaders, desperate to continue perpetuating the grouping of blacks, so fear people of color who espouse self-responsibility that they will do almost anything to undermine their message.

CONTRAST THE DONAHUE EPISODE to an interesting conversation I had shortly after I took control of the health products company in New Zealand. I had persuaded a young woman from North America ("Marilyn") to move Down Under and take the position of Operations Director. She was a very serious, confident, efficient individual who had a low threshold for nonsense. During one of our many conversations about life in New Zealand versus life in America, the question of racism came up. We were both impressed by how comfortable New Zealand was with the integration of its British conquerors and native Maori people.

Inevitably, the conversation turned to race relations in America and the question of political correctness in addressing black Americans. When I mentioned the term *African-American*, Marilyn grimaced and said, "I cringe when people refer to me as an African-American. I wasn't born in Africa; I don't know anything about Africa; I've never been to Africa; and I don't plan on ever going to Africa. So how do I qualify as an African-American?"

Good question. What Marilyn was expressing was a desire to not have her identity buried in a group, particularly a group she knew very little about. The need to be thought of in a collective way is about as far from the philosophy of rational living as a person can get.

To be sure, valid generalizations can be made about people based on sex, nationality, race, and, yes, even religious beliefs. For example, if you stated a self-evident truth such as American blacks, on average, tend to become professional athletes more often than do American whites, you certainly would be right. You also would be statistically right if you stated that American blacks, on average, tend to commit more violent crimes than do American whites. If you stated that Jews, on average, tend to become professional athletes less often than non-Jews, you would be right. You also would be right if you stated that Jews, on average, tend to commit fewer violent crimes than non-Jews. Because such generalizations are supported by hard facts, they are perfectly valid.

But let's look at these four examples from a more relevant slant. Approximately 99.9999 percent of American blacks are *not* professional athletes. Likewise, the vast majority of the American black population has never been found guilty of committing a violent crime.

What about Jews in professional sports? Well, as just one example, many people believe that Sandy Koufax was the greatest pitcher in major league history; Dolph Schayes is considered to be one of the fifty greatest National Basketball Association players of all time; and Sid Luckman, who played for the Chicago

Bears in the 1940s, is consistently named as one of the greatest quarterbacks ever. The list of Jewish *individuals* who have excelled in professional sports is pretty long.

Jewish criminals? How would you like to wake up one fine morning and find Meyer Lansky, Bugsy Siegel, or Mickey Cohen on your doorstep? These *individuals* operated outside the accurate generalizations about Jews and violent crime.

The point is that people can make true generalizations about groups to their heart's content, but such generalizations have no bearing on you, the *individual*. The more you glorify such factors

> Living a rational life is about individuals, not groups

as sex, race, nationality, and religion, the more you cloud your own individuality. Living a rational life is about individuals, not groups. Instead of fretting over what people say about "your group," use your energy to focus on *your* specific talents and *your* uniqueness. If you want the playing field to be leveled, do it by creating value, not through group force.

Above all, be careful not to become prey to any of the thousands of moral hucksters, tyrants, and charlatans who have anointed themselves leaders of one group or another. Acting on their rhetoric to throw in your lot with a group is a drastic move away from individualism. And it is the individualist who stands the best chance of achieving long-term happiness and success. The next time one of these unemployed powermongers organizes a protest march to demand special rights (under the guise of equal rights) for some group that presumptuously claims you as a member, do yourself a favor: Stay home and read a good book on individualism.

FREEDOM FROM HATRED

Racial hatred is not the only kind of hatred in the world, but it does serve as an extreme example of just how senseless, irrational, and self-destructive hatred can be. Unfortunately, the efforts of well-meaning people who counter this emotion by espousing love are for the most part misplaced. After thousands of years of urging people throughout the world to let go of their hatred, there is more animosity and loathing today than ever. Urging people to "stop the hating" has about as much impact as urging people to buy your product without telling them why it is in their best interest to do so. You cannot force someone to love another person. As history has repeatedly demonstrated, whenever force has been used to quell hatred, the hatred has rebounded many times over.

On the other hand, if, for example, you hated someone, and you asked for my input on the matter, I would appeal to your self-interest. I probably would submit a list of reasons why it is not in *your* best interest to continue hating the individual in question. My list would include such things as:

1. Hatred is a negative emotion that breeds negative thoughts, and negative thoughts produce negative results. Among other things, your thoughts attract other negative people, who in turn stir up your hatred even more. Elevated levels of hatred can drain you of emotional energy and poison your body.

2. Since the mind can focus on only one thing at a time, any time wasted on hatred is time not being used for constructive thinking, or at least pleasurable thinking. Hating is an extremely painful activity, and living a rational life calls for removing as much pain from your life as possible.

3. Ask yourself what the endgame of your hatred is. If there is no endgame—no purpose—what's the point? If your objective is simply to hate, then it becomes the height of irrationality, because your hatred is based on emotion rather than reason. Why use up valuable time-

and-energy resources to engage in a negative activity that has no definable purpose? Other than cases where people are prepared to use violence against those whom they hate—which, hopefully, is not your intent—hatred is usually an end in itself.

4. If your hatred for someone is based on something he did to you, the more time and energy you spend on hating that person, the more you allow him to hurt you. There is much truth to the adage that living well is the best revenge. Develop the habit of converting hatred into motivation to succeed, and let that be a blanket response to everyone you dislike. Success sets in motion a positive cycle. The more success you experience, the less time you have for petty matters like hatred.

5. Remember, getting what you want in life through rational living requires a conscious effort to make rational decisions. Therefore, since hatred is the most irrational of all emotions, it cannot help but to impede your efforts to achieve rational goals. Of course, if your ultimate objective is to commit violence against the object of your hatred, then your objective is in violation of another important aspect of rational living—"so long as the actions stemming from those decisions do not involve the use of force or fraud against anyone else."

Put another way, you don't have to love your enemies; just don't give them the satisfaction of hating them. If I were going to create the perfect human being, I would make one of his chief attributes the ability to instantly strike from his mind all thoughts of his enemies—including and especially all hateful thoughts—not just be-

> You don't have to love your enemies; just don't give them the satisfaction of hating them.

cause such an attribute would be virtuous, but because, from a rational standpoint, it would result in the achievement of more pleasure and less pain.

FREEDOM FROM GUILT

It is conventional wisdom that guilt is an unwarranted state of mind, which means there is never a valid reason for feeling guilty. But is this wisdom really sound? Guilt, according to one dictionary definition, is a feeling of responsibility or remorse for some offense, crime, or wrong, whether real or imagined. Therefore, there are two questions to address regarding guilt. First, who should define what constitutes *wrong*? Second, are you actually guilty of wrongdoing?

Who should define what constitutes wrong?

Tragically, a great deal of guilt is induced by the opinions and moral beliefs of others. There will never be a shortage of people who are happy to admonish you for doing something wrong. It's your job to make conscious, rational decisions for yourself, so never relinquish that task to others—especially strangers. When it comes to morality, in particular, you must lay down, and live by, a code of ethics with which you feel comfortable. Who among us has the knowledge and wisdom to qualify him to lay down moral guidelines for others? It is the character of *your* soul that should determine right and wrong for *you,* so long as your version of right does not include the use of force or fraud against anyone else. Let the character of the other person's soul guide his own actions.

Are you guilty of wrongdoing?

If, based on your knowledge of the facts and your personal code of ethics, you conclude that you have committed a wrong, then honesty and integrity compel you to face up to that fact and, to the extent possible, make reparations. At a minimum, an unequivocal apology is in order, which is an action that almost always engenders respect. In other words, guilt is a good thing to the extent you have a sound reason for feeling guilty, and provided it motivates you to take positive action.

One of the reasons one-third of Americans so detested Bill Clinton during the Monica Lewinsky debacle—and most of the other two-thirds disrespected him—was because he could not bring himself, of his own volition, to clearly and unequivocally apologize for his reckless and dishonest actions. It seemed pretty obvious, from watching and listening to the man on television, that the reason it was impossible for him to apologize was because his heart wasn't in it; i.e., he didn't feel a sense of guilt. Why? Because guilt requires a personal code of ethics. If a person is immoral—or even amoral—he will see no reason to feel guilty.

On the other hand, when an individual with a sound moral infrastructure is not guilty of wrongdoing, it is just as important for him to refuse to be burdened by guilt as it is to apologize and make amends when one is truly guilty.

To decide whether or not guilt is called for in any given situation, be sure to check the basic premises of anyone who admonishes you for wrongdoing. Personally, I believe that the most important premise overall is that it is never appropriate to feel guilty for trying to get what you want in life through rational means. In this vein, we've already been over the issue of so-called selfishness. But what about another media favorite—greed? Our illustrious education system admonishes kids not to be greedy, yet I doubt most educators even know what greed means. The most common dictionary definition of greed is *excessive desire*, which immediately brings forth a familiar question: Who has the right, let alone the wisdom, to decide what is excessive?

It's too bad that most educators possess neither the knowledge nor the intellectual honesty to teach youngsters that, in reality, it is excessive desire that makes the economy healthy. Excessive desire motivates entrepreneurs to create products and services that consumers want, as opposed to what politicians, bureaucrats, and self-styled consumer advocates think they should have. To produce such products and services, capital must be invested and workers must be hired, which in turn creates both wealth and a healthy economy. If this is the result of greed, then Gordon Gekko, in the movie *Wall Street,* was right: Greed *is* good.

Thus, anything that tries to restrain so-called greed—which includes most forms of business regulation—can justifiably be viewed as bad. Antibusiness politicians are greedy not for money, but for public applause and power, a greed that leads to abuses of the legal system, produces no useful products or services, and, worst of all, hurts, rather than helps, the economy. For those who are concerned about the unemployed, the solution is not to extend jobless benefits. The solution is to get the government out of the way so entrepreneurs can unleash their excessive desire.

In summation, unless you accumulate your wealth by defrauding little old ladies out of their life savings, economically speaking, you have nothing about which to feel guilty. On the contrary, you should feel proud that you are a net producer for society rather than a net consumer. Remember, looked at from a financial perspective, getting what you want in life is about creating value for others. Therefore, if you genuinely want to make the world a better place, keep your focus on achievement of your goals—*and don't feel guilty about it.*

FREEDOM FROM ENVY

Pretty much everything I said about hatred goes for envy as well. Envy goes hand in hand with the loser's syndrome of transforming desires into rights, because much misplaced desire stems from envy. There is a subtle difference between the terms *jealousy* and *envy.* Jealousy denotes a feeling of resentment toward someone who has gained or achieved something that one feels he instead deserves. Envy denotes a longing to possess something that someone else owns or has achieved.

Envy is the more perverse of these two negative emotions, because envy has nothing to do with success or failure. If someone thinks he deserves the promotion you just received, he may be jealous of you. But if he covets your new Mercedes because he's discontented with his ten-year-old Chevrolet, it would be wise not to leave your keys in the ignition at night. The latter, of course, is an example of envy.

At its extreme, envy becomes an obsession to destroy those who are more fortunate than you, an obsession that has fueled repeated social revolutions through the centuries, the most famous of which was the 1917 Bolshevik Revolution in Russia. This historic event led to seventy years of communist enslavement for hundreds of millions of people, and, in addition, wasted trillions of dollars on weapons and military preparation. This represented capital that could have been spent to increase production of goods and services to make life easier for the very people the system enslaved. Envy-based discontent is so intense that it allows the envious to justify virtually any action, no matter how heinous. Vladimir Lenin, leader of the Bolshevik Revolution, made no bones about this when he boasted, "To tell the truth is a petty bourgeois habit, whereas for us to lie is justified by our objectives."

In the event you have a trace of envy in your soul—and virtually everyone does—it is much to your advantage to work hard at trying to free yourself of this emotional disease. The more envious you are of others, the less likely you are to take constructive action with regard to your own life. Being envious of others is a monumental time-waster that no individual who is serious about improving his lot can afford, and the first step toward eradicating this mental menace is to understand how wealth is achieved through the creation of value.

Thus, those who are most envious are people who have not

discovered this truth, or, on having discovered it, are not willing to compete with others by creating value in the marketplace. A down-with-the-rich mentality, bolstered by a zero-sum view of wealth (i.e., where one person's gain is another person's loss), is an immature, almost childish view of the world. Nonetheless, this envy-based doctrine is continually being reinforced by university professors worldwide, particularly those who teach economics.

Every age has its "robber barons"—from Leland Stanford and J. P. Morgan to Howard Hughes and Michael Milken—and the devil of choice for our age is Bill Gates. Being the richest man in the world makes him an easy target for the envious. The reality, of course, is that Bill Gates is the world's richest man because he has arguably created more value for more people—particularly people of lesser means—than any human being in history. The measly billions he personally possesses pale in comparison to the uncountable trillions of dollars people have earned, and will continue to earn, as a result of his work. Gates and Microsoft have changed for the better the way we live, including those who don't even know how to use a computer.

The zero-sum-wealth perception is ignorance at its worst. The reality, of course, is that wealth creation is limitless. In the simplest of terms, if you make $1 billion this year and my income is zero, these two facts are totally unrelated. Further, and luckily for me, your making $1 billion does not affect my opportunity to earn as much as I possibly can in the marketplace. I am not limited by what *you* earn, but by my own ability and willingness to create wealth. What a neat reality.

Freedom from envy is a freedom that requires vigilance, because vote-hungry politicians and envious, disgruntled coworkers are constantly sprinkling our brains with its seeds. When you suspect this is happening to you, simply ignore any suspect comments, make it a point to thank any close-at-hand sprinkler for his "good intentions," then tell him that you won't be needing his services anymore.

I am convinced that the desire to impress others is one of the worst forms of mental imprisonment. It not only requires a considerable portion of a person's time and energy, it eats away at his self-esteem as well. There is nothing more degrading than knowing, whether or not it is consciously acknowledged, that you are saying something, doing something, or buying something with the primary purpose of impressing others.

True positive qualities such as dignity and civility are likely to be noticed by others, but these qualities should not be nurtured merely to make an impact on those around you. Your primary purpose should be to provide infrastructure for the soul. When I discuss being imprisoned by peer pressure, I'm talking about words and actions

> The desire to impress others is one of the worst forms of mental imprisonment.

that are intended primarily for the purpose of gaining the acceptance of others. The truth of the matter is that everyone, to one extent or another, possesses the tendency to speak and act in such a fashion. Even the most righteous among us is "on stage" from time to time, whether or not he consciously thinks about it.

Peer pressure begins in earnest in grade school, though the earliest stages can be seen in children years before that. It is a phenomenon that eats away at the personalities of youngsters year after year, all too often resulting in lost souls. Worse, millions of children have become fatalities—through such activities as drug use, drunk driving, and gang fights—as a result of yielding to peer pressure. Those who are lucky enough to survive their school years, particularly high school, usually begin the long road back to freedom from peer pressure in their mid-to-late twenties. Some are fortunate enough to travel this road rather quickly, others more slowly, and still others hardly at all. The longer it takes to achieve a reasonable degree of freedom from peer pressure, the longer a person experiences the internal humiliation of feeling like a grade-school child trying to impress his peers.

This dismal human trait cuts across economic barriers. Inner-city gang members strive for conformity and acceptance, expressed through violent behavior, as much or more than do suburban, midlevel executives vying for membership in the right country club. Indeed, eliminate the phenomenon of peer pressure and our prisons would probably be half empty. Ultimately, peer pressure evolves into self-pressure—motivation from within to impress others. In suburbia, this trait spawns affectation, the effort to make others believe that one possesses wealth or qualities he does not. People who are affected to an extreme have lost their identities. They are, in fact, the most imprisoned people on earth. While they feign dignity, it is a trait that, in reality, they totally lack. Affectation stems from an immature desire to "keep up with the Joneses," and having lived in suburbs in many cities throughout the world, I can assure you that this desire is systemic in the human race.

Conformity is nothing more than a method for achieving acceptance, and is usually a result of low self-esteem. The more a person focuses on gaining acceptance and popularity, the less he is able to focus on developing those things that bring acceptance and popularity as a natural consequence—such as strengthening his personal infrastructure and creating value for others.

FREEDOM FROM CAUSES

By the term *cause*, I am referring to any aggressive movement for the advancement of an idea or belief. Some of the more common causes we read about daily revolve around the environment, such as water conservation, saving endangered species, and preservation of the earth's rain forests, while others include such things as animal rights, abortion (for and against), euthanasia (for and against), homosexuality (for and against), and special rights for the handicapped, elderly, gays, and numerous other groups.

I am not against the existence of causes per se, because everyone certainly has a right to pursue whatever interests he so desires so long as he does not commit aggression in the process. Further, I have come to believe that there are many noble causes, the best examples of which are private charities whose financial records are open to the general public. In real practice, however, becoming involved in most causes fails the rational-living test in many ways, a few of the most important of which I have summarized below.

Wrongful Motivations

If you live long enough, you get the opportunity to hear about hundreds, or perhaps even thousands, of causes and to observe the people behind them. While one can always point to exceptions (such as the kinds of legitimate, noble causes alluded to above), the motivating factors behind most causes are sad reminders of the irrationality of being a professional cause advocate.

BOREDOM

High on the list of motivating factors is boredom. If you are supporting more than one or two (presumably noble) causes, it might be a good idea to go back and reread Chapter 2—several times. If anyone needs to get a life, it's a professional cause advocate. When the same names and faces keep popping up in conjunction with new causes, one cannot help but to wonder what some of these people do for a living. Observing a serial crusader like Jesse Jackson flitting from one picket line to another, volunteering his comments on why every problem in professional sports is a racial issue, and jetting from country to country to hug communists and terrorists, one cannot help but be curious about who keeps him in new suits, not to mention who pays for his plane fare and hotel accommodations.

In the words of the late social philosopher Eric Hoffer, "A man is likely to mind his own business when it is worth minding. When it is not, he takes his mind off his own meaningless affairs by minding other people's business."

GUILT AND ENVY

Both of these emotions play an important role in how much success a cause has when it comes to attracting new supporters. Get a person to feel guilty enough, or bring to the surface the envy that has long been simmering inside him, and the chances are pretty good that he'll support your cause.

SELF-RIGHTEOUSNESS

Self-righteousness is arrogance at its worst. I concur with Thoreau's view that very few people who claim virtuosity are really deserving of the mantle. We've already been over the problem of others wanting to set moral standards for you, so let me just underscore it with regard to causes: Living a rational life requires that you be in control of your mind, beginning with the construction of your own code of ethics.

> Just as it is arrogant for someone to preach morality to you, it is also arrogant for you to preach morality to others.

It goes without saying that just as it is arrogant for someone else to attempt to preach morality to you, it also is arrogant for you to preach morality to others—whether directly or under the guise of a cause. It is in your best interest to fight the urge to set moral standards for your fellow man, because not only does it tend to evolve into aggression, it takes time away from your working on improving your own moral structure. And it's *your* moral structure, not anyone else's, that will have a major impact on your ability to get what you want in life.

One factor that joiners of all but the most noble of causes have in common is a general ignorance of the facts. Arrogance and ignorance go hand in hand, from whence comes the expression *arrogance of the ignorant*. Given how often so-called experts turn out to be wrong in their predictions about the future, one might be justified in concluding that ignorance is almost a necessity for arrogance to exist. Environmentalists are notorious for this flaw, often hopping from one pet issue to another as new information surfaces that undermines their causes. Though there have been an endless stream of dire predictions about such things as overpopulation, depletion of the earth's rain forests, and ozone holes in the atmosphere, the world seems to go right on spinning, life expectancy rates increase each decade, and the standard of living, at least in industrialized nations, continues to climb upward.

LACK OF RESULTS

Not only are the motivations for becoming involved in causes questionable, but causes rarely achieve their goals. In fact, if causes had to rely on their track records alone, they would be lucky to attract any but the most bored, guilt-ridden, envious, self-righteous, and ignorant supporters. The most obvious examples of this are crusades to end war and poverty. Judging from 6,000 years of recorded history, poverty would appear to be a natural consequence of the ebb and flow of human events, particularly the result of government actions. Poverty is a subjective condition, but certainly we can all agree that extreme forms of poverty are found only where the most tyrannical forms of government exist. As we discussed, when men are free to pursue their own interests, value and wealth are created. In so-called democratic countries, no one who is willing to work is poor in the third-world sense of the word.

As to peace movements, short of self-styled wearers of white hats conquering every country on earth and holding in check those with aspirations to invade other countries, world peace is not possible. Crusaders can preach peace from the four corners of the earth to their heart's content, but their words have no effect whatsoever on the next Adolf Hitler, Josef Stalin, or Saddam Hussein. And for every evil person who today holds power, there are a thousand individuals as bad or worse waiting in the wings.

As noted in the Introduction to this book with regard to getting what you want through rational living, being anticrusade does not stop you from being kind, charitable, and civic-minded. On the contrary, having respect, and caring, for others is both noble and rational. It's simply that individual action is a more rational way to get results than group action.

Use of Aggression

Perhaps the most irrational aspect of all when it comes to getting involved in causes is that a significant percentage of them employ the use of force to achieve their ends. What actually happens in most cases is that cause advocates appeal to the government to force people to act in accordance with their desires. Oftentimes, this aggression comes in the form of lobbying government officials for special rights, but special rights for some always come at the expense of others.

By now this is familiar ground for you—aggression is in violation of the principles of rational living. Though most people have strong beliefs about one or more causes, such beliefs represent nothing more than personal opinions, and, as such, are morally inferior to individual liberty. If people are serious about living in a free society, liberty must be given a higher priority than all other objectives, including any and all causes that certain people may deem to be noble.

Unfortunately, there will always be misguided people in the world who arrogantly believe that achieving their desired objectives justifies virtually any means. This is especially true of those who sermonize about world peace, eradication of poverty, or such nonsensical abstracts as "the good of society" and "the public welfare." All too often, the endgame for the cause leader is repression of individual freedom. As Nobel Prize novelist and poet Anatole France so rightly pointed out, "Those who have given themselves the most concern about the happiness of peoples have made their neighbors very miserable."

LOOKING AT CAUSES from the standpoint of the individual who is serious about the task of achieving rational goals, I am moved to offer this simplistic version of Charles Dickens's first paragraph of *A Tale of Two Cities:* It was the best of times; it was the worst of times; it was, in fact, pretty much like any other time. In simpler terms, crises come and go, but none of them ever seem to bring the world to an end. (Of course, you'll never convince a dinosaur of that.)

Because of modern technology, this is even more true now than it was in Dickens' day. In fact, the most important element that professional cause advocates fail to factor into their crusade equations is technological advance. Technology not only renders irrelevant such perceived crises as the oil shortage of the 1970s, it also continues to raise the living standards of potential cause joiners. In our modern age of prosperity, nothing so irritates cause promoters—especially socialist cause promoters—as the realization that otherwise perfectly good prospects for their causes are relaxing in the backyards of their suburban homes, grilling steaks on the barbecue, and watching the kids splash around in their ten-by-twenty-foot swimming pools. Convincing these folks that they are being exploited by "the rich" is a very tough sell.

When the next crusader comes knocking at your door, babbling about this or that crisis, do yourself a favor and tell him to get a job, get out of the way of those who are creating value for others, and allow entrepreneurial genius to continue expanding the frontiers of modern technology and improving the living standards of people worldwide.

Using your time and energy to help promote a cause that advocates the use of force to make others accept an agenda that certain individuals feel is right is far removed from the objective of getting what you want through rational living. If you wish to make a serious contribution to world peace and prosperity, I suggest you use your time and energy to improve the one person over which you not only have meaningful control, but have the moral authority to control: *you.*

FREEDOM FROM POLITICAL PRESSURE

In reality, politics is nothing more than a hodgepodge of causes. The reason I'm granting it a whole section is because political causes ensnare so many otherwise rational people and have the greatest impact on our day-to-day lives. They serve as a collective model, as it were, for just about everything that is immoral and irrational about most causes, thus helping us to better understand the overall phenomenon of causes.

Political causes are insidious in nature because they have an air of legitimacy about them. People have been conditioned to believe that so long as a goal is achieved through the ballot box—which results in the use of government force—it is morally acceptable. What in fact occurs through the voting process can be best understood by examining the workings of an election.

In the United States, the heavyweight championship match of elections is the presidential election that takes place every four years. Thirty percent or so of the voters are at the conservative end of the political spectrum, while another 30 percent or so consists of hard-core liberals. Give both of these groups credit for one thing: No matter how misguided and misinformed they may be, they rigidly stay their course and demonstrate that they at least believe in something. These are the people you see on television, at conventions and pep rallies, wearing straw hats

180

bearing their candidate's names, thrusting cheerleading signs toward the sky, and grinning and shouting as though they had just won the lottery.

However, don't be too quick to scorn such childish behavior. The 40 percent or so of the voters in the middle—often referred to as "swing voters"—are even less admirable, because they have no philosophical or ideological beliefs at all. Swing voters can be swayed by almost anything, including a presidential candidate's good looks, engaging smile, or humorous one-liners—or simply his latest trip abroad. It is a source of never-ending amazement to me that whenever a president needs a boost in the polls, he need only climb aboard Air Force One and take off for a foreign country. As sure as day follows night, he can count on a certain number of swing voters thinking, "Golly, he sure does look presidential"—then letting the polls know, if asked, that they've decided he's a great president. I guess the reason ignorance is bliss is because it makes life so uncomplicated.

But even this nonsensical behavior is not the worst of it. Most swing voters are, plain and simple, for sale to the highest bidder. How right H. L. Mencken was when he opined that an election is nothing more than "an advanced auction of stolen goods." Each presidential candidate rushes from forum to forum, promising more government largesse to all who will step forward and cast their votes for him. Thus, the chief task of a candidate is to find a way to convince skeptical voters that he is the one who will actually deliver on the promised handouts. Don't buy into this game of shame; it's not the way to get what you want in life—and it's certainly not a moral or rational way to do so.

Since the two major parties' primary candidates rarely argue over premises (i.e., whether or not *any* government money—*your* money—should be spent on anything other than national defense and protecting the lives and property of citizens), they debate only how much money should be handed out and to whom. Doesn't every candidate promise to create jobs? Doesn't every candidate promise to fix Social Security? Doesn't every candidate promise to implement health care reform? Doesn't every candidate promise to fight poverty? Which means that, no matter how much loyalists protest to the contrary, at the end of the day it doesn't matter a great deal who wins.

Which in turn means that the United States really has a one-party system—the Demopublican Party—masquerading as a two-party system (Democrats and Republicans). Regardless of whom you vote for, you are casting a vote for the Demopublican Party. The reality is that the entrenched political system does not allow a president to take actions aimed at setting people completely free to look after their own interests. Republicans simply chase the tail of the Democrats by trying to outbid their free-lunch offers. Then, when they finally get elected, Republicans merely keep the status quo until the Democratic faction of the party can once again regain power and move their redistributionist agenda forward another step.

Following are just three of many examples I could offer as to why it is irrational, and thus an obstacle to getting what you want in life, to become involved in politics.

The Mandate Lie

The Mandate Lie, which flies in the face of rational thinking, is an integral part of the entrenched political system. Political-cause proponents, especially when it comes to presidential elections, love to remind citizens that the winning candidate has "the mandate of the people." In fact, no such mandate has existed in recent times. What in fact takes place in an election is that the two candidates of the Demopublican Party are propped up before the public, each candidate having been selected by a small group of politically active people.

Since approximately one-half of the eligible voters in the United States do not vote, and approximately one-half of those who do vote cast their ballots for the loser, roughly 75 percent of eligible voters have *not* given the president-elect a mandate. If you consider the fact that a significant percentage of people who voted for the winner did so only because they felt he was the lesser of two evils, this percentage goes even higher.

In truth, then, "mandate of the people" really means that a large majority of the people are ruled by a president for whom a small minority has voted. Some mandate.

Absurd Claims

The often ridiculous claims politicians make rely heavily on the failure of the masses to think rationally. In Chapter 3, I suggested that the reason approximately two-thirds of Americans thought Bill Clinton should remain in office, notwithstanding the fact that most of these same people realized he had engaged in criminal activity, was that it was a vicarious way of cleansing their own tainted souls. However, since it is reasonable to assume that not everyone who gave a thumb's up to Clinton's actions was guilty of criminal behavior or unfaithfulness to his spouse, there must have been another factor at work.

That other factor was the absurd but widely accepted notion that the president has the power, let alone the ability, to perform such miraculous tasks as "get the economy moving" and "create jobs." Firmly believing such nonsense, people felt it was in their best interest not to rock the country's financial boat. It was a case of ignorance overriding morality, i.e., "Reprehensible behavior be damned, I'm not going to do anything that might help kill the golden goose."

The reality, of course, is that no president can do anything to positively affect the economy other than do everything in his power to try to get the government *out* of the economy. As to creating jobs, the only way any politician can create a job is to take a job away from someone else, either directly or indirectly. By *indirectly,* I am referring to the fact that government-created jobs take money out of the economy and thereby cause other people to become unemployed. Government-created jobs are a result of government force, and force always interferes with the smooth workings of the marketplace. Since all government actions involve force, or, put more delicately, the threat of force, government can move the economy in only one direction: backwards.

An honest search for truth should reveal to any serious adult that it is the thousands of hi-tech entrepreneurs who have produced a booming economy and created millions of jobs worldwide. In reality, Apple Computer's Steven Jobs has alone created more legitimate jobs than all U.S. presidents in history combined. In fact, if you own a hot-dog stand, *you* have probably created more jobs than all U.S. presidents in history.

The truth of the matter is that how far man has advanced is not a reflection of his true potential; it is his true potential *minus* government interference. You should therefore carefully check the premises of any political cause before allowing yourself to be pressured into supporting it. The premise that a president can affect the economy in a positive way is ludicrous on its face, yet the vast majority of voters steadfastly believe it to be true. Why? Perhaps French philosopher Michel Montaigne said it best when he pointed out, "Men are most apt to believe what they least understand."

The Object Of Power

Joining a political cause to bring about social change is the height of naïveté. As history has repeatedly recorded, political revolutions, which are but extreme forms of political action, succeed only in reshuffling the power deck. When we talk about revolution, we normally think of basket-case countries such as Nicaragua, Uganda, and Ethiopia. We sometimes forget that industrialized nations such as France and the United States also have experienced revolutions.

The United States loves to romanticize the American Revolution, but are the people of Canada, New Zealand, and Australia any worse off for not having revolted against their British rulers?

The reins of power changed hands as a result of the American Revolution, but there is no reason to believe that U.S. citizens would now be less free or less wealthy if they were indeed citizens of the so-called British Empire. Of course, it's somewhat of a moot point, because by now the natural course of history has made Canada, New Zealand, and Australia independent countries anyway.

What in fact actually occurs in a successful revolution is that a new upper class emerges. The doors of elitism swing open, and new individuals (i.e., a small number of people, as opposed to the masses as a whole) rush to take their places inside, as Alvin Toffler describes in *The Third Wave:*

> Time and again during the past three hundred years, in one country after another, rebels and reformers have attempted to storm the walls of power, to build a new society based on social justice and political equality. Temporarily, such movements have seized the emotions of millions with promises of freedom. . . . Yet each time the ultimate outcome was the same. Each time the rebels re-created, under their own flag, a similar structure of sub-elites, elites, and super-elites.

What helps fuel revolutions is that millions of people are unable to achieve success in a totally free society, which motivates them to call for the use of force to make other people conform to their notion of freedom for all. There being no shortage of qualified freedom fighters throughout the world, someone is always happy to step up to the plate and lead a good-old-fashioned revolution. Almost without fail, of course, the result is that more people end up having less freedom than before, with Russia, China, and Cuba being well-known twentieth-century examples of this predictable scenario.

In other words, to paraphrase George Orwell, power is not a means to an end; power is an end in itself. The object of power is power. Those who buy in to the same old revolutionary themes discover this truth again and again, but their discoveries always come too late. In democratic societies, of course, revolution comes about through the ballot box, which saves a good deal of bloodshed. However, the promises and results are pretty much the same. The appeal is to middle-class and lower-class envy, while the most noteworthy result is a change in the power structure or a reaffirmation of the current power structure.

This being the case, why do we keep falling for copycat revolutionary themes? The answer is that we fail in our search for truth. Ignoring history, or being completely ignorant of it, we desperately and irrationally want to believe that what we love is true—and what we love most is the idea that a savior on a white horse will throw the bad guys out and hand us our "freedom." We want to believe that the smiling face on television can solve our problems so we won't have to take responsibility for our own lives. It is, of course, pure delusion. As historian-economist Thomas Sowell explains, "Everything is new if you are ignorant of history. That is why ideas that have failed repeatedly in centuries past reappear again, under the banner of 'change,' to dazzle people and sweep them off their feet." Or, in the words of Will Durant, "It may be true . . . that 'you can't fool all the people all the time,' but you can fool enough of them to rule a large country."

Without question, an educated electorate would be anathema for politicians. Politicians, however, need not fear an educated electorate becoming a reality any time soon, given that so many of our universities specialize in political and ideological misinformation. Don't take the bait on this all-important freedom obstacle. Use your rational powers to resist all forms of political pressure, especially the pressure to become involved in politics of any kind. It is the worst way I know of to get what you want in life, and as far removed from rational living as one can get.

CHOOSING FREEDOM

The response to the constraints of day-to-day life is often a little voice inside one's head that shouts, "Leave me alone!" This is why most of us relate so well to the theme song from the Broadway musical version of *Man of La Mancha,* as it does such a marvelous job of glorifying the elusive concept known as *freedom.* Don Quixote's words—*"I've got to be me . . . I've got to be free . . . I want to live, not merely survive"*—are enough to make one fantasize about quitting his job, leaving his possessions behind, and boarding a plane for some faraway paradise in the Mediterranean or South Pacific. However, since few people opt for such an exotic approach to achieving freedom, the next best thing is to be willing to pay the price of making the hard choices necessary to rid yourself of the major encumbrances in your life. And making hard choices is what the next chapter is all about.

TOUGH CHOICES

Principle #6: Develop the Self-Discipline to Act on Intellect Rather Than Impulse.

He who reins within himself and
rules passions, desires, and
fears is more than a king.

JOHN MILTON

A good rule of thumb to teach a young person is that for every minute of fun he has in his twenties, he should count on twenty-four hours of misery after the age of forty. This may be somewhat of an exaggeration, but it's wise to err on the side of caution when dealing with youthful minds that are inclined to be oriented toward instant gratification. "Living for the moment" implies that a person has little faith in his own future, while the act of foregoing comfort and pleasure today for a better life tomorrow implies belief in the ability to control one's own destiny.

Have you ever thought about how many choices you make in

a day's time? What's your guess as to the total number you make in a twenty-four-hour period—five, ten, twenty-five? Not even close. In reality, you make more choices every day of your life than you can count. When your alarm or clock radio goes off each morning, you choose whether to jump out of bed or pull the covers over your head. If you opt for the latter, every second you remain in bed represents a new choice you are making, so if you lie in bed for one minute, you're actually choosing at least sixty times to stay in bed. This decision-making process continues as you go through the ritual of getting up and getting out of the house. To shave or not to shave? To shower or not to shower? Which clothes to wear? What to eat for breakfast? Whether or not to watch the morning news? Whether to move fast or slowly?

As you can see, most of these choices are not of monumental importance. But others, such as decisions about love relationships, changing careers, or making an investment, can have a dramatic impact on your life. One of the most important keys, then, to getting what you want in life is to develop the self-discipline to make right choices. By *right choices*, I'm talking about rational decisions that will bring you happiness over the long term as opposed to decisions focused on bringing about instant gratification. So self-discipline is about restraining or regulating one's actions, repressing the instinct to act impulsively in favor of rational, long-term-oriented actions.

Regardless of the degree of importance, the fact of the matter is that everything you do throughout the day is based on choice. Many of your choices are made unconsciously, while others may require intense concentration over a long period of time. To the extent you put yourself on auto pilot and allow too many of those choices to be made unconsciously, you invite bad consequences into your life. On the other hand, consciously making rational decisions geared toward long-term, positive results dramatically increases your chances of getting what you want.

When I say that many choices in our everyday lives are made

without giving conscious thought to our decisions, I mean that we don't make a *conscious effort to make rational decisions.* Which means that we act on impulse a great deal of the time. Curiosity may have killed the cat, but impulsive action killed him, too. I know that to be a fact, because I've seem him lying motionless on the road, paying the price for having bolted in front of an on-coming vehicle. Cats act on impulse. Good news: You're not a cat. You have an intellect, and, contrary to what many people be-lieve, it is not against the law to use it. It's simply not a great idea for human beings to rely too heavily on impulsive actions.

Not long ago, while driving at a relatively high rate of speed on a well-traveled road, I spotted three young boys standing on the raised median strip, waiting to cross. Two of the boys darted across the busy street, having made the impulsive judgment that they could get to the curb before my car hit them. The third boy lunged forward slightly, then pulled back. If I could, I would have given him a high five and said, "Good choice." Immedi-ately after I passed the boys, the thought occurred to me that the odds of living a long, successful life were much better for the one who demonstrated self-control than for his two impulsive friends. We're always hopeful that our kids will be the ones to have the good sense not to go along with the crowd and take im-pulsive, dangerous action, because, as millions of people have discovered through firsthand experience, a single impulsive ac-tion can be fatal.

> Curiosity may have killed the cat, but so did impulsive actions.

Fortunately, most major decisions in our day-to-day lives don't have to be made in a split second. We normally have any-where from minutes to months to ponder our choices. Yet, "I didn't have a choice" has become something of a catchall excuse for making bad decisions. It is, in fact, an excuse based on self-delusion, because, no matter how unappealing your choices may be, you *always* have a choice. In extreme cases, one of your choices may be death, but, technically speaking, even that is a choice.

There is no worse feeling than being acutely aware that you should not be doing what you're doing, or, conversely, that you should be doing something you aren't doing. Whenever you find yourself in this kind of situation—and all people do from time to time, even those who are

> You always have a choice; choice equates to control.

generally self-disciplined—it's important to be conscious of the fact that you have *chosen* to do the wrong thing. To the extent you ignore this reality, you find it increasingly easier to focus on immediate pleasure, which in turn can result in a grim future.

A common example of people thinking they have no choice is to be found in the previous-investment trap. Have you ever invested an inordinate amount of time, emotional energy, or money in a situation that didn't work out? In this respect, a bad marriage or love relationship is very much like a bad stock investment. In either case, the attitude often is, "I've put so much into this situation that I have no choice but to see it through." If it's the stock market, such thinking can lead to one's losing a lot more money than he's already lost and later wishing he had cut his losses short. If it's a marriage or love relationship, the stakes are much higher, because staying in a bad relationship can mean many more years of pain. More investment capital can always be earned; time, however, is a fixed commodity.

It is a great comfort to know that you always have a choice, because choice equals control. Understanding this reality makes it easier to concentrate on making good choices, i.e., choices that are most likely to get you what you want over the long term.

HIGH CLASS VERSUS LOW CLASS

Everyone wants to be considered high class, but how many people take the time to think about what the term *high class* means? I guess to many people it translates into a big house, fancy cars, and fine clothes. To me, however, being high class equates to self-discipline—particularly the self-discipline to consistently resist the lure of momentary pleasure in favor of actions that one believes will produce long-term benefits for him and his loved ones. A low-class person, on the other hand, is someone who consistently chooses instant gratification over actions geared toward producing long-term benefits.

Thus, a high-class person merely does, on a consistent basis, what the majority of people know is right but choose not to do. I would therefore suggest that an excellent subgoal on the way to getting what you want in life is to *think* high class, because actions tend to follow thoughts.

Seed Planting

One high-class activity that will go a long way toward helping you to achieve your long-term goals is seed planting. As the words imply, seed planting is the philosophy of investing time, energy, and/or money today to reap benefits tomorrow. On a day-to-day basis, you don't notice that the seeds are slowly sprouting, but one fine day you wake up and discover that they are in full bloom. Seed planting is about laying foundations. It's about cultivating relationships. It's about planning and preparation. It's about investing time and effort today to be a step ahead tomorrow. Above all, it's about having the self-discipline to bypass instant gratification and make choices geared to long-term success.

Learning about computers has caused an increase in my appreciation for seed planting. I'm always surprised when I talk to someone who uses a computer, yet doesn't know how to create macros or templates. These two computer functions are classic cases of the efficacy of seed planting. Anyone can learn to create macros and templates in thirty minutes or so. Once learned, simple macros and templates can be created in a matter of seconds, complicated ones in a few minutes. Once created, a macro or template can be used thousands of times over a period of many years, saving untold hours of work. Put another way, the effort is measured in minutes, the benefit in hours. Unfortunately, it's been my observation that most computer users don't have a clue as to how much time they could save by learning simple procedures such as creating macros and templates.

Probably the most important seed-planting activity of all is learning. I find it fascinating that the older I get, the more important learning becomes to me, yet when I was in school, learning was anathema. I wish I had studied as hard in high school and college as I do now. As a writer, I plant an enormous number of learning seeds, and much of my planting is done on something akin to blind faith; i.e., I don't know when or if I'll ever need the newly acquired knowledge, but experience has convinced me that virtually everything I learn pays dividends at some future date—sometimes very far into the future. I never cease to be amazed at how often I use information I may have acquired ten or twenty years ago. The mind is a phenomenal filing cabinet that has a way of handing you the right file when it's needed, no matter how far in the past it may have been filed away.

Ironically, young people, who have most of their lives in front of them, have trouble exercising the self-discipline to plant seeds, but older folks, who are increasingly running out of time, are generally much more inclined to make long-term choices.

Life Maintenance

Being adept at avoiding problems goes a long way toward helping you get what you want, because the daily cares of life—those day-to-day unavoidable problems—provide more than enough challenge when it comes to achieving your goals. Another subgoal, then, on the way to achieving long-term success is learning how to avoid problems, which is best accomplished through "life maintenance." Life maintenance is really just another form of seed

> Learn how to avoid problems.

planting, but, unlike most seed-planting activities, its fruits are to a great extent invisible. Maintenance pays silent dividends in the currency of fewer and less severe problems. Unfortunately, it's hard for human beings to appreciate the absence of problems, which is why, as all marketing experts know, prevention is a hard sell.

Following are some specific areas of our lives where I believe it is particularly important to practice life maintenance in an effort to avoid problems and increase our chances of long-term success.

HEALTH

Unlike prevention, cures are very easy to market. In fact, a perfect headline to an ad could be:

I guarantee I can cure your cancer, without drugs, chemotherapy, radiation, or pain, within two weeks!

Of course, the person running the ad would have to close down his boiler-room operation on short notice, convert into cash the millions of dollars in checks he would receive, and find a way to get out of the country before being arrested. But rest assured that just about everyone afflicted with cancer would answer such an ad.

By the same token, we see thousands of ads, articles, and television shows each year that tell us how to *prevent* cancer, as well as heart disease and stroke, yet most of us choose to ignore them. Why? Because we don't have these diseases right now, so we aren't motivated to concern ourselves with them. It's so much easier to ignore the warnings and instead choose to indulge ourselves with cigarettes, liquor, and unhealthy food. After all, we can always worry about a disease when it arrives. Unfortunately, like most events, diseases have a way of intervening when we're least prepared to cope with them—and on short notice at that.

This is why a regular medical checkup—a way of making sure that the body's machinery is all there and still working reasonably well—is an essential part of health maintenance. So, too, are proper eating and exercise, because to be of any value they should be performed on a regular basis, preferably daily. There is, of course, no instant gratification in any of this. Is there anything fun about taking vitamins, flooding the body with juices, and eating fresh fruit for breakfast, salads for lunch, and steamed vegetables, tofu, and fish for dinner?

Of course, smoking is hands down the most destructive of all activities when it comes to body maintenance. Notwithstanding, millions of people push the health envelope by defiantly continuing to smoke. In Chapter 1, I opined that what keeps people smoking is the dangerous self-delusion that they are immortal. While this self-delusion is on an emotional level, on an intellectual level any smoker with an IQ above eighteen knows better. So what we have here is an overlap between a subconscious belief in immortality and a conscious lack of self-discipline. It is an overlap that can be quite deadly.

The fact is that people do have a choice when it comes to body-killing activities such as smoking, drug abuse, excessive alcohol intake, and regular consumption of foods heavily laden with saturated fat, cholesterol, and sugar. We've heard many celebrities—Yul Brynner and Sammy Davis, Jr., are two well-known examples that come to mind—appeal to the public to stop smoking after they themselves were diagnosed with terminal cancer. Their appeals were noble, but it's sad that their choices to ignore body maintenance cost them their lives. I find it helpful, when tempted to engage in a dangerous activity, to remember the messages of such people who have made avoidable mistakes—and lost. It is comforting to realize that I have the power of choice in such matters, and that I can choose to override the temptation to engage in life-threatening activities.

CHILDREN

Right up there with health maintenance is child maintenance. Talking to children when *they* want to talk is a critical activity of parenthood. Children have a different kind of mental computer than adults. They can go long periods of time without displaying the slightest hint of a desire to talk, then, at the most inopportune moment, desperately feel the need to share their thoughts. It's a major mistake to fail to put aside your cooking, television program, or business papers when your child expresses a desire to talk to you. If child maintenance is neglected too long, the child, to his parents' chagrin, may discover less constructive ways to satisfy the need to express himself.

ROUTINE

To many people, spontaneity is the ultimate symbol of freedom—do what you want, when you want, how you want. By contrast, routine—which is an integral part of life maintenance—represents a form of imprisonment to such people. Personally, I have found a routine to be an ongoing catharsis resulting not in imprisonment, but freedom. When my life is in order, I have more time to work on constructive, long-term projects, not to mention more time for pleasurable activities. The better one maintains a daily routine, the less his mind is clogged with petty problems, which in turn translates into lower stress and anxiety. In his book, *Ageless Body, Timeless Mind,* Deepak Chopra lists a regular daily routine and a regular work routine as two factors that retard the ageing process. A routine implies priorities, and priorities imply order.

MEDITATION/SPIRITUALITY

One of the highest priorities of a daily routine should be thinking time. By *thinking time,* I'm not referring to the kind of thinking one does at work. I'm talking about solitude, a quiet atmosphere (such as a park or beach), and a relaxed mind. Some refer to this kind of activity as "meditation." Others call it "Connecting with God." The label you give to it is inconsequential.

Viktor Frankl, in *The Unheard Cry for Meaning,* touches on this point when he offers an "operational definition" of God that he came up with at age fifteen: "God is the partner of your most intimate soliloquies. Whenever you are talking to yourself in utmost sincerity and ultimate solitude, he to whom you are addressing yourself may justifiably be called God." Frankl goes on to explain that such a definition avoids the dichotomy between atheism and theism, and that "If God really exists he certainly is not going to argue with the irreligious persons because they mistake him for their own selves and misname him."

In other words, what's important is not what you call it, or whether you're an atheist or religionist, but that you have the self-discipline to fit some sort of meditation into your daily routine. I am convinced that quiet reflection and contemplation comprise a major catalyst for successful endeavors. To accomplish such a state of mind, you have to have the self-discipline to avoid being distracted by meaningless thoughts, in particular mental chatter about petty, banal, and minor problems. It is also important, though much more difficult, to avoid focusing too much on immediate problems. Immediate problems represent the trees in your forest of possibilities. Most people are so busy pressure-cooking the problems of the moment that they simply don't have time to do creative thinking.

MAKING CONSCIOUS CHOICES

While we make many choices every minute of the day without consciously thinking about them, there are specific areas of one's life where it's important to make conscious choices in order to avoid the kinds of things that can become barriers to getting what one wants over the long term. Following are what I believe to be some of the most important of these potential barriers, and which therefore require special vigilance when it comes to practicing self-discipline.

Overcommitment

If you arbitrarily count life as beginning at age twenty-five (anything much before that being preparation for adulthood) and ending at age eighty, the average person lives 20,075 days. However, approximately one-third of that time is spent sleeping, while another one-third is spent on nonproductive life essentials such as getting ready to go to bed, getting up in the morning, attending to health and personal hygiene, and going grocery shopping. That leaves less than 7,000 days for the average person to do something constructive with his life.

Numbers don't lie, which is why they are a harsh reminder of just how important it is to make rational choices regarding how you spend your time. Most people go about their daily business as though they were going to live forever, wasting time with impunity on such activities as idle chatter, compulsively working on unimportant projects, and watching sitcoms, talk shows, and sporting events on television. All of which would be life-draining enough, but the activity that pushes the time-waster over the time-wasting edge is the making of extraneous commitments.

By *extraneous*, I am in the most general sense referring to commitments that are in conflict with the objective of getting what you really want. An activity such as exercise is relevant, because the evidence is conclusive that it increases your chances of good health and a longer life, and staying alive and healthy is a basic requirement for long-term success. Meaningful conversation is another relevant activity, because, by definition, it makes you a more knowledgeable and wiser person. Taking vacations is relevant, because it not only gives you short-term pleasure, but also relaxes the body, clears the mind for constructive thinking, and motivates you to work hard when you return home.

Commitments, on the other hand, have a tendency to fall into the category of irrelevant, a result of so many of them being made on impulse. Do you clearly understand the amount of time involved in joining an organization, and will the benefits more than offset your loss of time? Do you clearly understand the amount of time involved in committing to meet with someone on a business matter, and will the benefits more than offset your loss of time? Above all, do you clearly understand the amount of time involved in supporting a cause, and will the benefits more than offset your loss of time?

I mentioned earlier that it feels awful to know that you're doing something you shouldn't be doing right now. In this respect, for me the worst feeling of all has come from situations where I have impulsively made commitments, then felt obliged to follow through and make good on those commitments. The most effective way to avoid this problem is to develop the self-discipline to tell people who ask you for a commitment that you would like to think it over for a day or two. That doesn't necessarily mean that you're going to say no. It's just that a twenty-four to forty-eight-hour time period can, and usually does, mean the difference between making an impulsive decision and making a decision based on rational analysis of the facts.

It has often been said that one of the most certain ways to fail is to try to please everyone, and I concur with that belief. Intimidation and guilt are major factors here, because some people know how to lean pretty hard on their commitment targets. We've already discussed guilt, so that shouldn't be a factor in your decision-making process. Intimidation, however, can be a difficult weapon to combat. The truth of the matter is that intimidation, at its worst, borders on aggression, and you should make it a cardinal rule never to agree to anything that smacks of aggression.

What we're really talking about here is just another form of freedom—the freedom from being all things to all people. Unfortunately, it's a freedom few people ever achieve, notwithstanding the fact that they do have a choice in the matter. All other things being equal, when it comes to making commitments you should choose freedom by having the self-discipline to err on the side of caution.

Dishonest Actions

I've heard it said that if a person is honest, he doesn't have to consciously think about whether or not his decisions are on morally sound footing. I disagree. Granted, if there were such a thing as a totally honest person, perhaps he would have no need to think about his decisions. Such a creature, however, does not exist. Like it or not, virtually everyone, at one time or another, is guilty of deviating from his moral beliefs and engaging in situational ethics. Honesty, in other words, comes in degrees. There is no such thing as an honest or dishonest person. There are, however, people who are *basically* honest and people who are *basically* dishonest.

Therefore, assuming that you're neither a saint nor a hardcore, evil person, you fall into one of two categories—basically honest or basically dishonest. In either case, it is in your best interest to be conscious of your choices in all matters relating to honesty. To do this, you first have to make a mental and moral commitment to subordinate your desires to your values. Then, when your code of ethics is on the line, you have to have the self-discipline to follow through and make decisions that demonstrate that adhering to your values is more important to you than the current object of your desires.

> It's more important to do something because it's right than because you think others will approve of your actions.

A good rule to remember in this regard is that it's more important to do something because it's right than because you think others will approve of your actions. A person who is focused on adhering to his code of ethics in this way doesn't have to give much thought to how his actions will be perceived by others. Remember, most people do not love truth—and many even hate it—so choosing to do the right thing can sometimes feel uncomfortable to you. Also, never forget that you always have a choice, even if the right choice means that some people may become angry with you. Morality is not about pleasing others; it's about doing what's right. Nothing pays more handsome, long-term dividends than applying heavy doses of self-discipline where honesty is concerned.

Dispersed Attention

Another area of one's life where self-discipline is critical is when it comes to focusing on priorities. Setting priorities is relatively easy; sticking to them can be quite difficult. Compulsion is a factor here, because compulsion, as noted in Chapter 5, tends to cause one to focus on form rather than substance. All daylong, every day of your life, you make choices either to do what is most important at any given moment or to do something that is, at best, a lower priority. At worst, the activity of your choosing may be irrelevant, and focusing on irrelevant activities is not a great formula for success.

As a writer, I can tell you that it would be impossible to complete a book without consciously and constantly focusing on the task at hand. Writing is a lonely, ergonomically painful job, one that requires total concentration on the subject matter. To write well, one must be intense, which can be debilitating to the brain. The required intensity can become so great that I often find myself unconsciously searching for distractions. And guess what? I never have to look very far, because there are always more distractions than I can

> Every second spent on low-priority tasks is a second for which there is no refund at a later date.

handle close by. There is nothing quite as stimulating as dusting your work area, sharpening pencils, or programming numbers into your fax machine.

What usually saves me from working on such mundane chores is reminding myself that every second spent on low-priority tasks is a second for which there is no refund at a later date. You may not be a writer, but I can tell you without knowing your occupation that it is much to your benefit to think high class, which means making the choice to focus on your primary task at any given time and looking to the future to reap rewards. There is no better feeling than taking a vacation after success-fully completing a major project; there is no worse feeling than taking a vacation when you know that an important project has not yet been completed.

One of the most serious obstacles when it comes to focusing on top priorities is that most of us are in close proximity to people who are highly skilled in the art of time-wasting. I'm talk-ing about individuals who continually bombard you with gossip, side issues, petty matters, and irrelevancies. It takes a great deal of self-discipline not to allow such people to pull you off course. You also have to be vigilant when it comes to people who spe-cialize in setting up meetings. All other things being equal, and to the extent you have a choice, you should bypass as many meet-ings as possible.

In his classic novel, *East of Eden,* John Steinbeck emphasized the connection between working alone and creativity when he explained, "Our species is the only creative species, and it has only one creative instrument, the individual mind and spirit of man. Nothing was ever created by two men. There are no good collaborations, whether in music, in art, in poetry, in mathemat-ics, in philosophy. Once the miracle of creation has taken place, the group can build and extend it, but the group never invents anything. The preciousness lies in the lonely mind of a man."

The lonely mind of a man is precious, indeed. Einstein didn't discover his theory of relativity during brainstorming sessions with fellow physicists Hubble and Humason. The equations lead-ing to his discovery were conceived in solitude. To be sure, there were collaborations interspersed with solitary thinking sessions, but the theory of relativity was developed by one man.

The more meetings you attend, especially meetings set up by others, the more your attention is diverted from your highest priorities. If you're serious about achieving long-term goals, you must work hard at focusing on *your* priorities.

Assumptions

Some twenty years ago, my attorney and I had a conference call with an attorney (hereafter referred to as "Henry Dunce") repre-senting an audio-cassette manufacturer. In the past, we had talked privately about Henry's lack of legal skills and his pen-chant for irrationally defending his shoddy sentence structure and questionable word choices.

As the conversation neared its end, I realized that I would need to speak with my attorney alone. After Henry hung up, I told my attorney I would call him right back, to which he replied, "I'm in a hurry. Why don't we just finish up our business right now. Henry's off the line."

Indeed, I had heard a click after Henry said good-bye, and as far as I could tell there was no third-party noise on the phone, so I agreed to have our talk without first disconnecting our confer-ence call setup. It certainly was reasonable to assume that Henry was off the line, if for no other reason than it would have been to-tally unprofessional for him to remain on the line without our knowledge. As our conversation unfolded, my attorney com-mented, "Of course, Henry Dunce is so dense that we'll have to humor him in order to get this thing done."

Whereupon a voice—Henry's voice!—bellowed, "I am *not* dense, and I deeply resent your comment." Trust me, you don't want to hear the rest of the story. It was one of the most embar-rassing moments of my life, and one that taught me a lot about carelessly making assumptions. In the ensuing twenty years, I have taken part in many conference calls where I needed to speak with one of the parties afterward, but, no matter how pressed I or the other party has been for time, I've always exercised the self-discipline to hang up and call him back.

Assumptions, in general, are dangerous, and in some cases can be deadly. Among gun buffs, for example, there is an old, tongue-in-cheek saying when someone accidentally shoots himself that he was shot by an "unloaded" gun. No one in his right mind points a loaded gun at himself; it's always a case of someone *assuming* a gun was unloaded. Likewise, I am fascinated by how some people cross the street with a body language that borders on arrogance. They assume that because "the pedestrian always has the right of way," cars will automatically yield to them. You've probably seen the results of such an assumption lying in the crosswalk, with a police car and ambulance close by. What an ignorant and dangerous assumption for a pedestrian to make. The reason they call them *accidents* in the first place is that drivers don't always do what they're supposed to do.

I would not attempt to guess all of the reasons why the average person bases so many important decisions on unfounded assumptions, but I do believe that laziness is at least one factor. Certainly, my ill-fated conference call owed its ending to laziness on the part of both myself and my attorney. Caring is a wonderful antidote to laziness, because it's almost the antithesis of assumption. Show me someone who cares enough about what he's doing, and I'll show you someone who doesn't make many assumptions. Instead, he takes the trouble to check the facts out for himself.

On a day-to-day level, this laziness-leading-to-assumptions syndrome continually challenges us. I've found that life becomes much easier if I override my laziness with self-discipline even when it comes to seemingly innocuous matters. The classic example of how this habit can alleviate a lot of unnecessary problems is when it comes to dealing with repairmen. How many times have you had a technician or service person assure you that your VCR, computer, or some other appliance or electronic item not only has been repaired, but tested, only to find afterward that the item was not been properly repaired or that the repairs had created a whole new set of problems?

To the considerable irritation of repairmen, I'm adamant about testing the repaired item *myself* before they leave. Invariably, the item needs more work, after which I *again* test it. This won't make you popular with technicians or service people, but it's guaranteed to lower your stress. If you employ this kind of self-discipline to similar situations a thousand times a year, you can eliminate a considerable amount of wasted time and pain from your life.

Free-Lunch Temptations

Self-discipline will also help you repress the free-lunch urge in all its insidious forms. I say *insidious*, because free-lunch temptations are all around us, much more so today than fifty years ago. We live, in fact, in a free-lunch world, a world where most people truly believe in the artificial rights created for them by vote-hungry politicians. Succumbing to free-lunch temptations will prevent you from getting what you want in life, because it robs you of time, energy, and creativity that can be much better invested in activities directly related to achieving worthwhile goals.

The key to understanding that the free lunch is a fantasy is to recognize that you always have to give up something in order to get something in return. In modern parlance, we call this phenomenon a *trade-off*. I believe that the key to having the self-discipline to avoid the allure of the free lunch is to become a student of trade-offs. It is a subject that has long fascinated me, so much so that for many years now I have been able to instantly and automatically look for the trade-offs in every kind of situation that arises. If a seemingly good opportunity crosses my path, I immediately begin to look for the offsetting (and often hidden) negatives. By the same token, if I am confronted with a seemingly bad alternative, I automatically begin to look for the offsetting positives.

It is often situations that look the most positive that are really just free-lunch illusions. I'm not saying that great opportunities don't exist; it's just that you should make an effort to understand at the outset what the negative trade-offs are. Businesses regularly offer free bonuses in an effort to gain you as a customer, but such offers are not in the something-for-nothing category. A free bonus (such as an automobile manufacturer's factory rebate) is just a company's way of offering more value—a way of getting what *it* wants by giving you more of what *you* want. When I use the term *free lunch*, I am referring to situations where a person or entity offers to give you something (such as a welfare check) without your having to give anything in return (such as becoming a customer).

The best way to guard against free-lunch temptations is to continually search for truth, then employ the self-discipline to choose to do that which is in accordance with the truth you find.

CHOOSING ACTION

Many years ago, I happened to be at a hotel lounge in Palm Springs, California, with a friend. Without fanfare, the act for the evening was introduced—"Dionne," a stunningly beautiful, female singer. She bore a resemblance to the legendary Lena Horne, and carried herself with the style and grace of royalty. From the moment she began singing, patrons in the small lounge were mesmerized. In this unlikely venue, Dionne received numerous standing ovations, including several encores. I had never seen anything quite like it. There was no question in my mind that I was witnessing the birth of a star.

After finishing her act, Dionne sat at a table and chatted with some acquaintances. Being the young and impetuous tortoise I was, I scribbled a note to her on the back of my business card, inquiring as to whether she had a manager, then had a waiter deliver the card to her. As hard as it was to believe, she sent back a note saying that she in fact did not have a manager. After a couple of more notes back and forth, I set up an appointment for Dionne to meet with me in my office later in the week.

Our initial meeting went very well, and, after a couple of weeks of negotiations, I succeeded in signing her to a management contact. Among other things, the contract called for me to finance a demo tape, arrange for the production of a record album, and use my marketing skills to promote her talents. In the course of filling out a variety of forms, Dionne told me she was thirty-two years old, which surprised me, because I had guessed her age at about twenty-seven or twenty-eight. I wondered why someone with her beauty, presence, and, above all, remarkable voice was not already a household word. Thirty-two was hardly old, but a bit late to be getting started in the entertainment business.

Dionne explained to me that she had studied classical music in college, but had not pursued a career, opting instead for marriage and the life of a traditional housewife. Then, one day, she made up her mind to act on the words of Don Quixote—*"I want to live, not merely survive"*—and thus began a belated singing career. Hers was not an emotional decision, but an intellectual one. She described the hunger she had felt inside for so many years, believing that her destiny was far different from the way her life had thus far unfolded. She knew that she had been given a gift at birth, and a little voice from within kept telling her it was wrong not to use it.

But the most impressive thing Dionne said to me was in response to my warnings about how tough the music business was and how fickle and unpredictable the public could be. In a characteristically self-confident manner, she smiled and told me that if she never became famous, if she was relegated to playing in small lounges the rest of her life, it wouldn't matter to her, because she was doing what she loved. The stage, no matter how small, was her world, and an appreciative audience, no matter how sparse, her reward. I was totally impressed with her purist attitude and passion for singing.

As things progressed—cutting a demo tape, making an appearance on a national talk show, and preparing for an album—it occurred to me that, considering the large investment I was making in Dionne, I had better take out a life-insurance policy on her as called for in our contract. Inexplicably, she wavered a bit, but she had no choice but to take a physical. However, when it came time to fill out the insurance application form, she asked if she could first speak with me in private, so we set up a time for her to come to my office.

When Dionne walked through the door, she brought a surprise along with her—two surprises, in fact. Make that two *very tall* surprises. I assumed that one of the twin towers was her boyfriend and the other his acquaintance, so when she introduced them as her *sons,* I nervously chuckled and waited for a more serious introduction. Alas, her first introduction *was* a serious introduction. Still in a state of shock, I asked everyone to sit down and enlighten me as to what this was all about.

Almost everything Dionne had told me was true—her study of classical music in college, initially playing the role of the traditional housewife, then pursuing her destiny as a singer, and the fact that she had no manager. The part of the story that changed, however, was her age. Given that I had thought she looked younger than the thirty-two years of age she admitted to, it would be an understatement to say that I was not prepared for her real age. Knowing that she was required to put her age on the insurance application, Dionne had decided she would first break the news to me in person. As it turned out, she was not thirty-two, and certainly not in her late twenties as I had originally supposed. Dionne was *forty-seven years old*—a female Methuselah! Put another way, she was a medical miracle.

After the paramedics revived me, Dionne, her twin-tower sons, and I had a warm chat, saturated, as you might have imagined, with insider jokes about her age. The twin towers particularly liked my tongue-in-cheek barb about taking Mom on the road and making a fortune by having people place wagers on her age. I suggested that if we got started right away, we could all be rich before Dionne was confined to a nursing home.

As things turned out, my relationship with Dionne lasted only about a year, chiefly because I couldn't afford to continue the level of investment I felt was required. The music business gives new meaning to the term *dirty,* and it became apparent that, notwithstanding Dionne's talent, it was going to be a long, hard road to the top—and long was something that was in very short supply in her case. When we parted ways, Dionne reaffirmed her feelings about not caring if she ever became famous and being satisfied just doing what she loved. I haven't seen her in more than twenty-five years, and the thought that she is now seventy-two years of age is unfathomable to me. And so is the thought that she may now look almost forty years old.

The point of this little tale was to dramatically demonstrate that a person can choose to take radical action and totally change his life if he wants something badly enough. What each of us must overcome—and, indeed, what Dionne did overcome—is a phenomenon known as *homeostasis.* Homeostasis, in loose psychological terms, is the tendency to live with existing conditions and avoid change. It is a tendency that all human beings possess to some extent. Homeostasis contradicts the universe, because the heavens are in a constant state of change. In addition, each of us continuously changes physiologically from birth to death. Nevertheless, most of us persistently resist major changes in our lives, and self-discipline is needed to overcome this potentially self-destructive problem.

While change for the sake of change can be harmful, or even counterproductive, change based on rational thought can breath new life into a life laden with frustration, boredom, and/or despair. Dionne knew in her heart what was right for her,

"And now, ladies and gentlemen, my latest and greatest discovery—
the young, the beautiful, the exciting . . . Dionne!"

but I believe that's true of most people. What made her unusual
was that she had the mental toughness to choose to change the
course of her life and take action. I would be surprised if she isn't
still on stage, still smiling, still knocking 'em dead, still getting

standing ovations by the bushelful in small lounges across the country.

IF YOU'RE CURRENTLY in a dead-end domestic or work situation, or perhaps unhappy about where you live, a major change for the better is yours for the choosing. Major change can be scary, because the unknown is a dark and mysterious place, but not as scary as a lifetime of pain. If you know the truth about your present situation, and the truth is not to your liking, then the question is, Do you have the courage and self-discipline to make choices that are in accordance with that truth?

Remember that if you can't muster the self-discipline to take action, inaction also has consequences. To the extent you are guilty of the latter, you will have no choice but to *react* to changes as they occur. The problem with reacting to life's inevitable changes, however, is that you're always dealing from a position of weakness. On the other hand, when you are proactive—when you exercise the self-discipline to effect beneficial changes in your life—you deal from a position of strength. There are, of course, no guarantees. Your actions could turn out to be wrong, but at least they will be *actions* rather than *reactions*.

> A major change for the better is yours for the choosing.

Changing jobs, going into business for yourself, moving to another city, terminating an unworkable marriage or love relationship, or just about any other kind of major change one can think of is within your grasp. The key is to open your mind to truth, then be willing to move beyond your past conditioning and look at possibilities you may have previously refused to consider.

Everything I've talked about in this chapter, and, indeed, in this entire book, is of little value to you without action. In effect, making choices is synonymous with action. Self-discipline, however, refers to the act of choosing to do that which you have already determined is right, i.e., that which is in your long-term best interest. So it's not action we're after, but *self-disciplined* action. Whether it's your search for truth, creating value, maintaining a good attitude, building character, eliminating undesirable people from your life, freeing yourself from activities that imprison you, or any other noble objective, making tough choices that are in accordance with what you already know to be right is crucial to success.

> Take *self-disciplined* action. You can't afford to passively allow the future to arrive.

You can't afford to passively allow the future to arrive; getting what you want in life through rational living requires the self-discipline to properly prepare for it.

INJUSTICE FOR ALL

Principle #7: Learn from Bad Breaks,
and Move On.

The dice of God are always loaded.
—RALPH WALDO EMERSON

One of the toughest things about life is that there are no guarantees. You can do everything right—consistently discover truth, create value for others, develop a strong personal infrastructure, eliminate negative human forces from your life, free yourself from unnecessary constraints, and employ self-discipline in your daily affairs—yet have all your efforts offset by one bad break. Life, in other words, can be unjust. Learning how to overcome life's injustices is a crucial aspect of getting what you want.

A fatalist, be he an atheist or religionist, would tend to believe that injustice is predetermined. In the case of the atheist, however, an injustice really represents a random event; i.e., the fact that it was predetermined by the so-called Big Bang is pretty much irrelevant, because the bottom line is that he didn't know it was going to happen. On the other hand, a religionist would tend to believe that an injustice is the work of God, possibly as a punishment for some wrongdoing. The reason for the injustice is not always clear to him, though it's possible that it may become clear at some future time. If not, the religionist can also choose to believe that the reason for the injustice will become clear in the afterlife.

INJUSTICE FOR ALL

Regardless of the reason for a perceived injustice, the first thing one must determine is whether or not it is, in fact, an injustice. In other words, when it comes to injustice, you have to check your premises to make certain your perceptions are correct. If a person's belief system is faulty, his premises also will be faulty, which in turn ensures false perceptions. The best example of this would be a person who is caught up in the folly of victimization. Such a misguided individual would tend to see the world as unjust.

Thus, just having an improved grasp of reality—a result of simply improving one's search for truth—can remove a great deal of injustice from a person's life. Given that there are so many real injustices in life, it is decidedly not in your best interest to create additional, artificial injustices to add to your emotional burden.

Following are some of the more common injustices that I believe one has to learn to overcome if he is serious about achieving long-term happiness and success.

Introduction to Injustice

Most people's first awareness of injustice comes early in school. School is a microcosm of the injustices that lie ahead in adulthood. Few children are lucky enough to make it through school without experiencing shattered dreams, smashed egos, lowered self-esteem, and many other traumas of varying shapes and sizes.

If we lived in a kind, just, rational world, schools as we know them would be outlawed. Children start going to school normally between four and six years of age, most of them happy little things eager to interact with other children. Unbeknownst to them, however, painful injustice is about to enter their lives. The standard bearer of the child's coming bouts with injustice is a larger-than-life figure they immediately come to know as "Teacher."

All too often, Teacher is someone whose major objective is to put in her twenty-five years with as few problems as possible, then start collecting her pension. Anathema to Teacher is anything that makes waves, anything that causes her twenty-five-year journey to Pension Heaven to be more eventful than necessary. Her greatest obstacle in this pursuit is the ultimate wave-maker, the angry parent. Teacher can handle bad kids, but an angry parent can become an unmanageable problem.

Injustice in school comes in many forms, but one that hits home hardest is when a good-hearted, friendly child comes face to face with a bully. Going back to the days of Father Flanagan of Boys Town fame, it's been popular to say that there's no such thing as a bad child. Every parent, of course, knows better. There are, in fact, kids in every school who derive great pleasure from inflicting pain—particularly mental pain—on other children. These are the little sweethearts I like to refer to affectionately as *NLKs* (nasty little kids). Anyone who wonders how NLKs come into being need only attend a parent-teacher meeting to find out. They say that the apple never falls far from the tree, and when you see an NLK's parents, more often than not they are NHBs (nasty human beings).

NLK's are not a problem for the focused-on-retirement teacher, because she knows she can keep them in line by simply overpowering them. However, parent problems set in when an NLK starts picking on a nice kid whose only sin is that he wants to be friendly and have fun with the other children. "Johnny," nice kid and naïve to the core, reports the NLK's misdeeds to Teacher. The NLK, of course, denies any wrongdoing, and Teacher smoothes over the matter in the hopes that it will somehow go away.

No such luck. The NLK, delighted that his bullying went unpunished, goes after Johnny with a vengeance. Johnny again reports the NLK's bullying tactics to Teacher, who now is starting to feel the early warning signs of a parent wave. In the hopes of stemming the tide, Teacher admonishes both the NLK *and* Johnny to behave, then sends them on their way.

By now, the NLK is ecstatic. He could care less about getting in trouble himself, but he's over the moon about having the power to get that little goody-two-shoes Johnny in trouble. Now it's time to step up his attacks, both physically and verbally. The result? This time Teacher, highly agitated by the wave that is growing ever stronger, admonishes only Johnny!

Finally, Johnny's parents, frustrated over hearing daily tales of their son's being bullied, decide to visit the principal of the school. The principal listens to their concerns, then sets up a meeting with Teacher in her classroom. This results in a friendly little chat among Teacher, principal, Johnny's parents, and Johnny, at the end of which Johnny's parents are assured that the school does not, and will not, tolerate bullying. As Johnny's parents say their good-byes, Teacher displays her best Saddam Hussein smile, thanks them for sharing their thoughts with her, and assures them that there will be no more problems.

First-time parents leave the school naïvely believing that they now have the full support of both the principal and Teacher, and are relieved to know that their child is going to be safe. Unfortunately, Teacher has other ideas. Feeling comfort in the fact that the teachers' union has filled her basket to the brim with artificial rights, one of which is that it would take an act of God to fire her, stays up half the night thinking of sadistic ways to get

"How thoughtful of you to stop by and share your thoughts with us. You can count on my watching Junior very closely from now on in class."

even. She clearly sees Johnny's parents as a serious threat to her otherwise peaceful ride to retirement.

Charged up from a night of planning, the next day Teacher admonishes Johnny in front of the entire class, pointing out that apparently Johnny doesn't want to get along peacefully with the rest of the class, and bringing Johnny to a state of tears in front of his classmates. This humiliation tactic sends a message to the other children, nice kids and NLKs alike, that Teacher doesn't like Johnny and that he is therefore fair game. As a result, at recess and lunch time other NLKs enthusiastically join the original NLK in bullying Johnny. When Johnny complains to Teacher, he quickly learns about a reality of life called "strength in numbers." Everyone who took part in the bullying session agrees that it was Johnny who started the trouble. Result? Teacher, of course, pretends to believe them, and punishes Johnny.

If you're a parent, you know the rest of the story. It never gets better. Johnny's parents are now left with three options. They can uproot Johnny, put him in another school, and brace for a new wave of NLKs. They can continue to complain to the principal, knowing that this is certain to result in Teacher's finding new and more insidious ways to exact retribution from Johnny. Or they can leave Johnny in school, keep their mouths shut, and let him be battered day in and day out by the NLKs, who now know that Teacher fully supports their acts of aggression.

Johnny, once a happy, loving, self-confident child, has now experienced full-blown injustice at the tender age of six. Welcome to the world, Johnny.

WE'RE TAUGHT EARLY ON that "Sticks and stones will break my bones, but words will never hurt me," but it's hard for a child who is being ostracized to believe it. The saddest person in the world is the child who is told, "You can't play." Or the child who is chosen last, then greeted with negative comments such as, "Oh, no, not you," from the other children on his side. Of course, if teachers did their job on playground duty, painful experiences such as this would not occur. Thus, it's not the cruelty of children that makes such injustices possible, but the lack of supervision by teachers who spend recesses and lunch hours gabbing with each other about the latest movies they've seen, their upcoming vacations, or last night's television game shows instead of fulfilling their playground responsibilities. In this respect, bullied children are really victims of negligent teachers.

Because of the apathy on the part of most teachers to make school a safe and happy environment for all children, it's up to parents to carry the ball and explain to little minds that even though justice is the norm, there is, and always will be, injustice in the world. That being the case, rather than sheltering a child from truth, it is much to his long-term advantage if his parents prepare him for the real world. Coping with injustice is an important survival skill if a child is to grow into a well-adjusted adult.

Even more important is teaching children that they have the ability to overcome most of the injustice they will encounter throughout life. For example, an adult can combat a routine injustice such as slander (the adult version of sticks and stones) not by lashing out at his slanderers, but by making certain that his own hands are clean, conducting himself with dignity, and focusing on his own success. Likewise, a child can be taught to overcome bullying, exclusion, and putdowns by holding his head high, refusing to engage in cruel actions himself, studying hard and getting good grades, and rigidly abiding by the rules. In other words, children should be taught that results are the best antidote for injustice.

> Results are the best antidote for injustice.

Unpunished Evil

From the standpoint of the average, law-abiding citizen, one of the most troubling and frustrating kinds of injustices is unpunished evil. We've all seen people engage in acts intended to harm others, sometimes even criminal acts, yet escape without suffering any discernable consequences.

The last decade of the twentieth century saw two of the most spectacular cases of unpunished evil in modern times—the O. J. Simpson trial and the failed impeachment trial of Bill Clinton. Both had far-reaching effects on people not just in the United States, but in countries around the world. The bottom line to most individuals, regardless of whether they were for or against either of these men, was that two people walked away from their crimes without punishment. This sent a signal, particularly to young people, that criminal activity does not necessarily result in bad consequences. It also reinforced in our minds that the world is full of injustice, so what's the point in trying to live an upstanding life?

The similarities between these two cases have been well documented by the media. Aside from the fact that both men escaped punishment, the attorneys for, and supporters of, both of them managed to switch the focus of their trials, the O. J. trial being transformed into the trial of Mark Fuhrman and the Los Angeles Police Department, and the Clinton impeachment trial being transformed into an investigation of special prosecutor Kenneth Starr and the president's so-called political enemies.

The O. J. trial, of course, could be explained away by the fact that a near all-black jury simply ignored the evidence (jury nullification) and acceded to attorney Johnny Cochran's pleas to put Detective Mark Fuhrman and the L.A.P.D. on trial. The Clinton trial, however, seemed to have a much greater impact on the public. Earlier I discussed why a majority of Americans wanted Clinton to remain in office. First, many people saw it as a way of cleansing their own tainted souls; i.e., "if the president isn't punished, then the sins I've committed must be okay, too." Second, there was a misguided notion that Bill Clinton was somehow responsible for the booming economy created by Bill Gates and other value-oriented entrepreneurs, thus they were willing to overlook his criminal activity for the sake of protecting their own financial interests.

But what about the other one-third of the American public? Though it was never given much press, the fact is that an awesome 40–50-million adults wanted the President of the United States thrown out of office—or worse! Since I'm apolitical, I observed the Clinton story with a certain degree of detachment, my interest being primarily from a psychological and sociological viewpoint. From this perspective, I found it to be a most fascinating study. Over a period of time, I recorded the views of about

200 people, most of them friends, acquaintances, and business associates.

Contrary to more scientific, professionally conducted polls, my informal survey produced no more than a half-dozen people who thought Clinton should remain in office. Further, with few exceptions, the mere mention of Clinton's name evoked extreme anger and revulsion—in many cases, even hatred—in a majority of the people with whom I spoke. Why such uncontrollable wrath for a man whom the majority of citizens supposedly wanted to remain in office?

What I found was that most people's harsh feelings were not the result of the Monica Lewinsky affair, or, for that matter, any single incident. It was the overall perception that Bill Clinton had been lying and committing crimes throughout his entire political career, yet had never received any punishment. Further, Clinton's day-to-day deception incensed people—bombing innocent civilians in an attempt to get the media's focus off of his personal problems, holding hands with black ministers and singing hymns in an inner-city church immediately following his forced admission about the Monica Lewinsky affair, instantly changing his laughter to sadness when he realized the cameras were on him as he left his "friend" Ron Brown's funeral, and, of course, his memorable, Broadway-caliber performance when he waved his finger at the American public on national television and emphatically denied everything.

In other words, many people strongly believed that Clinton's sexual exploits in the White House were the least of his sins. From the alleged rape of Juanita Broaddrick to the sexual advances made to Paula Jones and Kathleen Willy ... to Travelgate ... to the Whitewater debacle ... to Filegate ... to allegedly giving the Red Chinese top secret technology ... to the suspected murder of potentially harmful witnesses, they assumed, rightly or wrongly, that Clinton had committed every imaginable kind of crime, all without punishment. Worst of all, they were bothered by his uncontrollable habit of flaunting his success every time he escaped justice. (Interestingly, and as a side note, I found that the vast majority of anti-Clinton people in my informal survey harbored even stronger negative feelings about Hillary Clinton than they did about her philandering husband.)

Whatever the facts may be, and whether you supported or detested O. J. Simpson or the Clintons, is not the issue. What's important is that millions of people are still convinced that in both cases evilness went unpunished, and to these people the outcomes of the O. J. and Clinton sagas mattered a great deal. The harm of perceived unpunished evil is that it can poison a person's mental processes with negative emotions such as hatred and frustration. In addition, dwelling on unpunished evil can be an enormous time-and-energy-wasting activity.

It is said that all that is required for evil to triumph is for good men to do nothing. But the corollary—that good men taking action will overcome evil—doesn't appear to always work in the real world. I am not suggesting that you should have no interest in helping to protect society from criminals. What I am suggesting is that you should come to grips with the reality that evil actions do often go unpunished, which is part of the bigger problem that life in general is filled with all kinds of injustices. Thus, given that high-profile cases such as O. J. Simpson and the Clintons are far removed from your life, you should not allow them to consume a significant portion of your time-and-energy resources.

Interestingly, Dr. Andrew Weil, in his book, *8 Weeks to Optimum Health,* urges readers to avoid reading or watching the news several times a week in order to lower their stress. Many people claim they are apathetic about negative events in the news, but in reality it is almost impossible not to be affected by them. As one grotesque injustice after another is splashed across our television screens and the front pages of our newspapers, the best way to protect your psyche from their negative impact may very well be to act on Dr. Weil's advice.

It is also important to recognize that whether or not the perpetrator of an evil act has gone unpunished is a matter of perception, and in this regard the O. J. case serves us well. While it's true that O. J. Simpson escaped the death penalty that many people felt he deserved, it is entirely possible that his life today has become a living hell. For example, from what we know of the case, it seems clear that his oldest daughter, Arnelle, knows that he murdered his ex-wife and Ron Goldman. Can you imagine how you would feel every day of your life if you had brutally murdered two innocent people and one of your children knew it? And what about Simpson's fear that his younger children will eventually read up on the case and discover the truth? Can you imagine living under the threat of that kind of emotional time bomb?

In addition, O.J. Simpson is a sociopath whose entire life had revolved around public adulation. What must his life be like since that adulation turned to hatred? How does he feel when he walks into a restaurant and people get up and walk out? What's it like for him to have people yell, "Murderer!" when he walks down the street with his children? What goes through his mind when his old pals don't speak to him? On top of all this, there are no more television-commercial offers, no more celebrity party invitations, and no more Brentwood mansion. While O. J. appears to be leading a carefree life of golf and fun times with his two younger children, he may very well be dying a thousand deaths every day of his life.

When Good Things Happen to Undeserving People

Right up there with unpunished evil as a source of frustration is the pain caused by having to watch good things happen to people whom we perceive to be undeserving. It's a frustration that tends to divert your attention from focusing on things that can most contribute to your getting what you want in life.

This is where one has to be careful not to delude oneself by confusing wishes with reality. People who feel victimized tend to perceive the success of others as unjust, with jealousy playing no small part in the matter. At worst, envy can set in, and we've already covered the dangers of harboring envy in one's soul.

Some years ago I hired, through an acquaintance, a professional speaker ("Bill") to make a presentation to a group of business people. I was very impressed with Bill's performance, and subsequently employed him on a couple of other occasions. Following one event, he and I went to a hotel coffee shop to wind down. At some point in our conversation, he got around to talking about his career and the professional speaking business in general.

Bill described himself as a "journeyman speaker," and lamented that even though he knew he was much better than many well-known speakers, he had not been able to make a breakthrough to the $7,000–$10,000 speaking-fee range. I sympathized with his frustration, because I believed him to be much better than a number of high-profile speakers whom I had seen perform. To make his point, Bill asked me if I had ever heard of a certain speaker (hereafter referred to as "David Warner"). I answered that I had only a vague recollection of his name. He then told me that he was going to send me an audio album Warner had recorded, and that he wanted me to give him my feedback.

About a week later, Warner's album arrived in the mail as promised. Within a day or two, I got around to listening to it, and was shocked at what I heard. On a scale of one to ten, I gave this supposedly top speaker a one. It sounded as though he was reading his material from a script, and not doing a very good job of it at that. Though I knew his album had been very successful, to me it was shallow and trite, and I found him to be embarrassingly dull.

A couple of days later, Bill called to see if I had received the album. I answered in the affirmative and told him straight out that Warner wasn't even in his class, and that he was, in fact, a very poor speaker. Bill explained that Warner was something of a

226

joke among professional speakers, and that, worst of all, he was arrogant about his inexplicable success.

How was it possible that Warner could command $10,000 for a speaking engagement, while Bill was lucky to get $2,500— that is, when he was able to land a speech at all? He explained that Warner had all the proper credentials—the top college degrees, a distinguished military background, a reputation for being religious and family-oriented, and more. Because he had come along at just the right time, recording an album that an audio-cassette company decided to back with a heavy marketing effort, Warner had been able to combine his successful album with impeccable credentials and parlay them into a successful speaking career. Though his lack of speaking skills was well known throughout the industry, his success seemed to have taken on a life of its own. In other words, David Warner was what is commonly known as "an accident of history."

In Bill's eyes, this was a classic case of good things happening to an undeserving person. It was such a grave injustice from his perspective that he couldn't even talk about it without exhibiting a great deal of emotion. I haven't seen Bill in years, but I still vividly recall how deeply he allowed Warner's success to bother him.

I've often wondered if Bill's frustration could conceivably have been an underlying cause of his own inability to break out of the pack and become a name speaker. Even though I agreed with his assessment of both his own talents and Warner's lack thereof, he had allowed the negative emotion of jealousy to steal too much of his valuable time and energy. Of course, neither I nor anyone else could ever prove that Bill's frustration had negatively impacted his career, but, regardless, his story is enough to make one leery of expending too much time and energy thinking about the success of others.

In all likelihood, you've felt the same as Bill at one time or another about some individual who has achieved seemingly undeserved success. After all, just knowing someone who was born into a wealthy family is enough to cause the injustice banner to be raised. I also think that a large percentage of the population feels that it's unjust for professional athletes—particularly illiterate, mean-spirited, and/or arrogant athletes—to be paid millions of dollars a year to jam a basketball through a metal hoop, outrun tacklers on a football field, or hit a baseball over a fence. In this regard, the late exobiologist Carl Sagan made an interesting point when he rhetorically asked why schools didn't award letter sweaters to students who excelled in science and the arts rather than sports. He felt that the message being sent to children—that sports are more important than academics—was unhealthy, and I'm inclined to agree.

The same complaint is often heard about decadent rock stars, so-called rap performers, and even actors. Perhaps the cruelest blow of all is that the marketplace determines precisely how much value these people create, and rewards them accordingly. The problem is not with the marketplace, since the marketplace is merely a way of measuring value, and that measurement is based on the combined, subjective opinions of millions of people. The real problem stems from the misplaced priorities, lack of taste, and absence of virtues of those who vote in the marketplace. In other words, it's a societal problem rather than a marketplace problem, and honesty compels me to admit that even the belief that it's a problem is a matter of personal opinion.

Thus, whether it's a famous person, a competitor, a fellow worker, or a casual acquaintance, you can count on good things sometimes happening to people whom you believe to be undeserving. The bad news is that there is absolutely nothing you can do about it. You may be repulsed by rock "music" and rap, but the market for such entertainment is unlikely to change much in your lifetime. The fact that people in these fields are bathing in fame and fortune is an injustice only in the eyes of the beholder. The solution isn't to fret about it; it's to make sure that you don't use your own time and money to increase the demand for such people's services. To feel disdain for marketplace choices is perfectly natural; to dwell on the perceived injustice of such choices, however, will get in the way of your getting what you want.

When Bad Things Happen to Good People

Bob Connell, a high school classmate of mine, was a superbly conditioned athlete who was into healthy eating long before the general public even knew there was such a thing. He was self-confident, and always appeared to be in control of his destiny. Best of all, he was a terrific guy, easygoing and friendly to everyone.

In college, Bob seemed headed for greatness. He was on the swimming team, and doing well academically. His future looked bright. Then one day came the news. A Trans World Airlines Super Constellation had collided in midair with a United Airlines DC-8 over New York City. Bodies and the wreckage of the two aircraft had been strewn over a wide area of the city, with the DC-8 crashing into a heavily populated section of Brooklyn. It was a gruesome scene that the major networks covered in graphic detail. Shockingly, Bob Connell had been aboard the Trans World Airlines flight.

At Bob's funeral, the pastor emphasized what a full life he had lived in a relatively short period of time. He talked about the usual things ministers emphasize when someone dies unexpectedly, and said that God had his reasons for taking this young man so early in life. On the way out of the church, another classmate of mine who had attended the funeral service angrily said to me, "I don't care what the pastor says, the truth is that Bob just got screwed."

That comment stayed with me for a long time. Did Bob Connell just "get screwed," or was there a reason for his untimely death? In the ensuing years, I, like everyone else, have become aware of numerous other instances of seemingly good people being victims of harsh death or disabling injuries. Why was Ron

Goldman brutally murdered when he was in the midst of doing a good deed by bringing Nicole Simpson her glasses? Why did Christopher Reeve end up a quadriplegic as a result of merely riding a horse? Each of us could make a long list of similar injustices, not only regarding people we have read and heard about, but individuals we personally know. Nonetheless, as with good things happening to undeserving people, dwelling on such injustices can seriously hamper our efforts to achieve great things.

> Dwelling on injustice can hamper your efforts to achieve great things.

I HAVE LONG BEEN FASCINATED by how timing seems to play such a major role in determining whether a person's life ends in disaster or success. People who were born at the wrong time in the old Soviet Union lived bleak, terror-filled lives under a brutal dictatorship, sometimes being sentenced to hard labor in the gulag, other times being put to death. Jews who happened to have been living in Germany and other Nazi-occupied European countries during Hitler's reign experienced an even worse fate. People living in Hiroshima or Nagasaki in 1945 became victims of the first atomic bombs dropped on a civilian population.

Good may ultimately triumph over evil, but what about the millions of people who don't live long enough to benefit from the triumph? For them the triumph of good comes too late. Why do certain people become victims of evil, while others are fortunate enough to be born at a different time in the same geographic area? Professional black athletes in America live in luxury, but their ancestors were kidnapped, sold into slavery, and spent their lives in misery. How can life be so unjust? When we witness or read about these kinds of injustices, it raises the age-old question: Why? To anyone who believes in God, the question is even more specific: Why does God allow such evil to exist?

A *Time* magazine article some years ago reflected on this very question. If God exists, the author rhetorically pondered, why does he permit evil in the world? The article alluded to such perceived evils as Hitler's attempted extermination of the Jews, the recent cyclone in Bangladesh, the plight of the Kurdish refugees, and Pol Pot's use of the Khmer Rouge to kill some 2 million Cambodians. It thrashed over much of the same ground covered in Harold Kushner's book, *When Bad Things Happen to Good People.* Forced to reconcile his belief in God with his son's tragic death from the incurable, rapid-aging disease progeria, Rabbi Kushner arrived at the interesting conclusion that God is all-loving, but not omnipotent.

Though it would be impossible for most of us to view this topic from Rabbi Kushner's perspective, I feel it is spiritual fudging to say that God is a good guy, but impotent. Playing with semantics is pointless; either God is all-knowing and all-powerful, or He is not God.

The *Time* article paraphrased theologian Frederick Buechner in pointing out the dilemma that you can match any two of the following propositions, but never all three: (1) God is all powerful. (2) God is all good. (3) Terrible things happen. In George Smith's book, *Atheism: The Case Against God*, he states the dilemma in more detail by writing, "Briefly, the problem of evil is this: If God does not know there is evil, he is not omniscient. If God knows there is evil but cannot prevent it, he is not omnipotent. If God knows there is evil and can prevent it but desires not to, he is not omnibenevolent. If . . . God is all-knowing and all-powerful, we must conclude that God is not all-good. The existence of evil in the universe excludes this possibility."

To Smith's persuasive list, however, I would add one other possibility: God knows there is evil in the world, but does not choose to stop it for reasons that are beyond our understanding. In other words, God alone knows why He does what He does. If God exists, He is unknowable and undefinable by human standards. *That* is what makes him God.

The *Time* article goes on to say that "Perhaps man is to God as the animals of the earth are to man. . . . Can it be that God visits evils upon the world not out of perversity or a desire to harm, but because our suffering is a by-product of his needs?" Well put. However, to extend this analogy and look at it in a slightly different light, consider the possibility that man is to God as a dog is to man, and a dog is to man as a flea is to a dog; i.e., the man, the dog, and the flea, who are merely tagging along for the ride, have neither the faintest idea as to why their masters do what they do nor the means to ever know.

The question then becomes: Is God indifferent to us, as the dog is to the flea, or does He allow us to suffer for reasons we do not understand? When someone takes his dog to the veterinarian, the dog has no idea why his master allows pain to be inflicted on him. In the same way,

> Accept evil as a part of life, but don't dwell on it.

perhaps God doesn't always give us what we want, but what He knows we need.

One could even take the position that it's the height of arrogance to suggest that we should be able to understand evil and suffering, let alone make judgments about the actions of a Supreme Being. If there is a God, surely he operates in a completely different dimension than us, thus He alone knows His purpose. Therefore, even though *Atheism: The Case Against God* is an undeniably brilliant book, its impeccable logic is rendered irrelevant if God does, in fact, exist; i.e., Smith's logic is valid only in a secular dimension. A Supreme Being would transcend secular knowledge, just as man transcends a dog's capacity to understand human reasoning.

It therefore seems inconsistent to believe in God, yet question perceived evil. Only God can know the reasons for the existence of evil. On the other hand, if one is an atheist, he has no choice but to accept random evil as a natural aspect of life. The

bottom line is that the most profound search for truth will never yield a conclusive answer to the question of why evil exists. It therefore makes sense to accept evil as a part of life, do the best you can to stay out of its way, and focus your efforts on positive pursuits that have the potential to bring you ever closer to achieving your goals.

Illusory Injustices

Earlier I discussed how faulty perceptions can lead to one's erroneously perceiving something to be an injustice. But even if one's perception of the facts is correct, it is still possible to erroneously conclude that a bad circumstance is an injustice. The problem is that we tend to judge events on the basis of their immediate impact, but, as life repeatedly teaches us, the long-term consequences of an action can be quite different from what we initially observe. The bad is superficial and obvious; the good often takes investigation and long-term observation. In other words, the true result of an event may take a long period of time to come to fruition, thus our initial conclusion may be an illusion.

For example, though many people believe that evil went unpunished in the cases of O. J. Simpson and the Clintons, their conclusion does not take into account the future. Additionally, there are both atheists and religionists who believe that the ultimate punishment comes in the afterlife. Anyone who believes either in bad karma or in God's meting out punishment after death has no grounds for jumping to conclusions as to whether or not an evil has gone unpunished. So long as we're alive, none of us can ever know for certain what the final chapter holds.

Interestingly, the phenomenon of short-term illusions is as true for good breaks as it is for bad breaks. As one makes his way through life's peaks and valleys, he often finds that getting the sweetheart, job, or opportunity he believed he always wanted turns out to be the worst thing that could have happened to him. Thus, just as there are always offsetting positives in every negative situation, so too are there offsetting negatives in every positive situation. In truth, virtually every experience we have is both good and bad, thus the individual who is adept at seeing the good in bad and the bad in good is certain to be more successful in maximizing pleasure and minimizing pain than someone who sees only one side of the good/bad coin.

It is also important to examine your own actions when trying to determine whether something is a true injustice, because often what a person perceives as a bad break is really nothing more than the natural consequence of his own actions. When this occurs, we are victims of an illusion. At work here is the self-destructive habit of employing transference in an effort to avoid accountability. Bad choices lead to bad results, not injustices. To the extent you improve your skills when it comes to searching for truth, and have the mental toughness to act according to the truth you discover, injustice becomes less of a problem in your life—which translates into increasing the odds of getting what you want.

Daily Cares of Life

Fortunately, most of the injustice we encounter in our daily lives is not of major importance. The day-to-day injustices that find their way into our affairs could be more properly categorized as the "daily cares of life." These are the little irritants—bad breaks, as it were—that gave birth to Murphy's Law, especially the part that states, "If anything can go wrong, it will—at the worst possible moment." They also are the little irritants that can be overcome by anyone who is intensely focused on a goal and determined to attain that goal at almost any cost.

In this regard, I know of no better example than that of an inventive neighbor of mine in New Zealand, John Britten, who built a futuristic motorcycle in his garage. John, a quiet, unassuming, totally focused individual, set a goal to win the prestigious Battle of the Twins international cycle race in Daytona Beach, Florida.

Building his cutting-edge cycle involved over 6,000 parts, most of which John hand-made. With the notable exception of the engine, John's extraordinary bike was constructed primarily of carbon fiber, a first for the motorcycle industry. He had dedicated helpers who worked for free, mostly at night, while holding down full-time jobs during the day. Incredibly, the actual cost of John's masterpiece was not more than a few hundred dollars, while many large corporate sponsors spent several million dollars on their entries.

Working while others slept was a Britten norm that was accepted by those who agreed to become involved in his projects, to the point that toiling around the clock became his trademark. Anything short of a superhuman pace would have made it impossible for him to build his one-of-a-kind cycle from scratch in just under eleven months, barely finishing in time for the Battle of the Twins race.

With just three weeks to go before the big race, John's carbon-fiber cycle crashed while being tested. It was a cruel blow, a bad break that everyone agreed John didn't deserve. The task of locating and correcting the problem, then repairing the bike, seemed insurmountable, but John and his crew again managed to overcome all obstacles and arrive in Daytona just in time.

But during the qualifying run, disaster again struck. Just twelve hours before race time, a hairline crack in a cylinder sleeve—one of the few parts John had not built himself—threatened to end his bid for the unofficial world championship for twin-cylinder motorcycles. John's reaction? After tireless but fruitless efforts to find the right spare part in the Daytona area, John, who had no previous experience in welding cylinder sleeves, repaired the broken sleeve himself.

By race time, John had been awake forty-seven hours since landing in Daytona, but, as events unfolded, it looked as though the monumental effort of the Britten team would finally pay off. But once again, like a scene out of a depressing Hollywood script, bad luck reared its ugly head. With John's cycle leading the pack, rain forced an end to the race one lap from the finish, which necessitated that the race be run over again from scratch.

In the restarted race, John's cycle again led the pack most of the way, until—you guessed it—yet another non-Britten-built part, a faulty rectifier, halted John's bid for victory once and for all. John Britten had captured the admiration of the racing world, but had failed to come home with a trophy. When he returned to New Zealand, however, he didn't waste time focusing on the bad breaks he had experienced in Daytona. Instead, he went right back to work, rebuilt his unique motorcycle, and returned to Daytona the next year. This time, he finally won the Battle of the Twins championship, a Rocky Balboa finish if there ever was one.

John Britten didn't just create entertainment value, but product value as well, with the first commercial version of the Britten motorcycle selling for a record $140,000. Not a bad return on the few hundred dollars he had spent on the design and construction of the original model.

The moral to this story is that most bad breaks, particularly those that do not involve life-changing injury, terminal illness, or death, are no match for human intervention. As Benjamin Disraeli once said, "Man is not the creature of circumstances, circumstances are the creature of man. We are free agents, and man is more powerful than matter." Intangibles such as focus, commitment, action, and determination, all of which John

> Most bad breaks are no match for human invention.

Britten possessed in abundance, have a way of rearranging the playing field, notwithstanding injustices harsh enough to bring most of us to our mental knees. John Britten proved that a determined, focused individual can overcome most of the bad breaks one encounters in life.

Ironically, though John was a master at overcoming the daily cares of life, shortly after winning the Daytona title—in the prime of his life at age forty-four and hard at work on a revolutionary new airplane—he was diagnosed as having cancer of the liver. Mercifully, he passed on quickly, but it was a very sad ending for those who knew him.

IT'S ALL A MATTER OF PERSPECTIVE

A few years ago, I was staying in one of Houston's nicer hotels while in the city on business. After a tiring, stressful day, I made an appointment one evening for a massage at the hotel's health spa. By the time my appointment rolled around, I was in a pretty gruff mood and looking forward to having someone work on my tired body.

As I finished putting my clothes in a locker and wrapping a towel around my waist, a spa worker greeted me and asked that I follow him to my assigned massage room. It crossed my mind as a bit unusual that the masseur himself hadn't come out to greet me, but, being exhausted and stressed, I didn't give it a great deal of thought.

After entering the massage room, the masseur introduced himself, shook my hand, and asked me to lie facedown on the table. As I began to get onto the massage table, I happened to notice that the masseur was staring straight ahead. I immediately did a mental double take, then instantly was jolted out of my own little myopic world. It was evident that the masseur, "Paul," was blind.

I soon felt comfortable enough to ask him if he had been blind all his life. "No," Paul responded, "it happened about thirty years ago, when I was nineteen years old." He went on to explain that he was planning to become a doctor, and was attending a summer orientation session at a special training school for a few weeks. Paul became friendly with a fellow who took him into his confidence and told him about a lucrative scam he was operating. The man had a ring of college students cashing fake bank checks he had printed up, and was giving them a percentage of the take.

After a time, he asked Paul if he would like to get in on the scam. Paul immediately said no, and thought that would be the end of the matter. But later that night, the scam operator came to Paul's motel room and pulled out a gun. He told Paul he had no choice but to kill him, because he knew too much about his illegal activities. Without even offering Paul an opportunity to promise never to mention it to anyone, the man shot Paul in the head. He assumed Paul was dead, and left him lying on the floor in a pool of blood.

The bullet severed Paul's right optic nerve. He was later told that his left eye could have been saved had he been taken to a hospital right away. Instead, he laid on the floor for eighteen hours before he was found, and blood clotting and other complications caused him to lose the sight in his left eye as well. In a voice of resignation I will never forget, Paul concluded his tragic story by saying, "I've been blind ever since."

I suddenly found myself thinking of all the things I take for granted that Paul had never experienced. In his entire adult life, Paul hasn't seen a beautiful tree, a spectacular sunset, or a magnificent painting. Lying on the massage table, my fatigue and stress seemed to fade away as these sobering thoughts pervaded my mind. How right Socrates was when he said, "If all our misfortunes were laid in one common heap whence everyone must take an equal portion, most people would be contented to take their own."

> Not every bad break is negative in the long term; not every problem is an injustice; and not every injustice is of major importance.

An important element in getting what you want is the ability to keep problems in perspective. Not every bad break is negative in the long term; not every problem is a bona fide injustice; and not every injustice is major when juxtaposed against the millions of injustices that occur daily throughout the world.

Prevalence of Handicaps

A healthy perspective has allowed me to view so-called physical handicaps in a different light since my daughter was diagnosed with multiple sclerosis at a relatively young age. Like most parents confronted with the illness of a child, I went through the usual stages of denial, anger, and despair. However, as the years passed, I increasingly focused on how lucky my daughter was that she did not have chronic-progressive multiple sclerosis. People with chronic-progressive multiple sclerosis deteriorate rather quickly, and usually become confined to a wheelchair early on. My daughter, who is attractive, smart, and personable, has been able to lead a relatively normal life, raise a child, and continue on a successful career path. Knowing that there are millions of people much worse off than my daughter has had a positive impact on both of us.

Technically speaking, a handicap is any kind of disadvantage that makes success more difficult. Indeed, over time I have come to realize that every person born into this world has at least one bona fide handicap. An obese person has a handicap; a person with attention deficit disorder has a handicap; a person with a low IQ has a handicap. Handicaps can be developed after birth or can come into one's life in the form of an inherited environment. A dislikable personality is a developed handicap; an abusive parent is an inherited-environment handicap.

You, too, have a handicap; in fact, you probably have several of them. I don't know what they are, but I know you have them. Everyone you meet, no matter how successful or happy he may appear to be, has a cross to bear. No one makes it through life without feeling the unjust pain of a handicap. Like it or not, however, we must each play the hand we've been dealt. We can't go back to God and ask that the cards be reshuffled.

The fact that everyone possesses a handicap of one kind or another is a healthy insight for any conventionally handicapped person to think about. From Helen Keller and Franklin D. Roosevelt to Stevie Wonder and Stephen Hawking, the evidence is clear that physical handicaps—the epitome of injustice—can be overcome. Remember, a handicap is a disadvantage that makes success more difficult, but there's a big difference between *difficult* and *impossible*.

> There's a big difference between *difficult* and *impossible.*

Attitude and Handicaps

Unfortunately, many people with developed or inherited-environment handicaps have trouble coping. A tragic example of the latter is "Vince," an individual I came to know briefly while working on a business project some years ago. Vince was the ultimate all-American boy—handsome, genius IQ, and personable. In high school, he was a straight-A student, star quarterback of the football team, and the object of attention from the prettiest girls. Unfortunately, he inherited an environmental handicap—alcoholic parents.

To my surprise, the very first time I met Vince he psychologically disrobed himself. He not only told me about his alcoholic parents, but explained that, as a result of his upbringing, he was totally "screwed up"—unreliable, unambitious, and unable to see any project through to completion. I detected a great deal of self-pity in Vince, and even guessed that he subconsciously enjoyed playing the role of the all-American boy who let everyone down.

I COULDN'T HELP but compare Vince's handicap with the handicaps of millions of other people who have enjoyed a great deal of happiness and success. The difference, quite obviously, is that Vince was never able to come to grips with his handicap, whereas many others, with far more serious handicaps, have been able not only to come to terms with their handicaps, but overcome them.

One such person was my longtime friend, Jim Blanchard. Jim lived a rational life perhaps more than any other person I've known, totally in accordance with universal principles. Whenever I feel like I might be babying myself, I think of Jim as a source of inspiration.

As a teenager, Jim was tall and handsome, and he believed in individualism at an age when most kids don't even know what the word means. One evening during his senior year in high school in New Orleans, Jim and two of his buddies were drinking heavily at a dance, then made the mistake of driving when they left. It was raining heavily, and there were no seat belts to speak of in those days.

One of Jim's friends was behind the wheel, doing what teenagers usually do when they're drunk: speeding. Flying down St. Charles Avenue at seventy miles an hour, the car failed to negotiate a curve in the road, flew up in the air, and slammed into an oak tree. Jim, who had been in the backseat of the car, was catapulted through the air like a human cannonball. His flight came to an abrupt halt when his body hit a light pole at full speed. In that instant, at the tender age of seventeen, Jim's life was forever changed.

He vividly recalled a priest giving him his last rights at the scene of the accident, but that proved to be premature. Jim woke up in Charity Hospital, and immediately knew something was very wrong. He had no feeling in either of his legs. An intern broke the news to him that his spinal cord had been severed in three places and he would never walk again.

Things went from bad to worse. His girlfriend of nearly three years, who had been away at college, came to see him in the hospital. His happiness over her visit lasted only until she told him that their relationship was over, because she had fallen in love with someone else at college. Jim was devastated. How much awful news could one person handle in such a short period of time?

After a long hospital stay, Jim's parents took him to a rehabilitation center where he spent several months. His first night there, he recalled saying to himself, "I can beat this thing. I'm going to beat it."

When Jim finally came home, he found two understandably doting parents who wanted to do everything possible to make him comfortable. Though he loved his parents dearly, their overprotectiveness bothered him a great deal, so much so that he decided he had to prove to himself that he could become independent. He had heard about a special program in Mexico where paraplegics and quadriplegics could share houses together and learn to become self-sufficient. After some investigation, he made the decision to go to Mexico and begin the long process of turning his life around.

Living with four other men in wheelchairs, one of whom was a quadriplegic, was an eye-opening experience for Jim. He learned to take care of his own personal needs, and developed a camaraderie with the other men. It was an experience he told me he would never forget. When he returned to New Orleans after about five months, having proven that he could take care of himself, he was anxious to get on with his life.

He finished his senior year of high school, then earned a college degree. A major turning point came when a friend gave him copies of two Ayn Rand classics, *Anthem* and *The Fountainhead*. These two books set the tone for what was to become an almost legendary career in free-market business activities.

The rest of Jim's story could fill a book, because he lived life to an extent that would be difficult for most people to imagine. In 1971, he invested $50 in a coin business, which ultimately became a $115-million precious-metals and rare-coin company. In 1986, he sold his company to General Electric Capital Corp. for enough millions to make him independently wealthy for life.

Jim traveled more than anyone I've ever known, and did just

about anything and everything one can imagine. When a mutual friend told me that he and Jim had gone mountain climbing, I asked him how that was possible. He responded, "Because Jim doesn't understand that he's crippled." No sentence could better have described the essence of Jim Blanchard.

When an indescribably painful event intervenes in a person's life, as it did in Jim Blanchard's, he has two choices. He can feel sorry for himself and give up, or he can get mad. Jim chose to get mad. He realized that it's the mind, not the body, that makes the decision to pick yourself up, brush yourself off, and continue on in the face of overwhelming odds. Jim may not have been able to pick himself up physically, but he instinctively knew that nothing could stop him from picking himself up mentally.

I'm sure that if Jim could have had the power to undo the terrible accident that forever changed his life, he would have done so, but he knew that wasn't reality. So, rather than fighting pain, he accepted the hand he was dealt, and in fact wondered whether he would have been as successful had he never been in that fateful accident many years earlier. Jim learned to play his cards wisely, knowing that fate sits on the other side of the table plotting future injustices.

Sadly, after a vigorous and successful life, on March 20, 1999, Jim Blanchard died unexpectedly in his sleep at age fifty-five. I will always miss him.

MOVING ON WITH LIFE

Other than terminal illness, accidental death, or a dire situation such as being in a concentration camp, there are very few things in this world that can prevent you from transforming your dreams into reality. Whether or not you carry on in the face of adversity is determined not by your body, but your mind. You should therefore make it a habit to think in relative terms and focus on the abundance in your life rather than the negatives. And whether or not you believe it, there *is* abundance. Make it a top priority to discover your assets, nurture them, and use them as they were meant to be used.

Luckily, injustice is just one aspect of life. Therefore, though injustice is painful, it is best to accept it as a natural part of life, handle it as quickly as possible when it occurs, then move on. Learn to view every problem, every bad break, every injustice as just another rite of passage.

Interestingly, but sadly, my classmate who said that our mutual friend Bob Connell "just got screwed" by being on the wrong airplane at the wrong time ended up taking his own life some years later. While it would be a leap to suggest that an obsession with injustice was the motivating factor in his suicide, I have often wondered if his anger over Bob's unjust fate wasn't indicative of a mind too focused on the negative side of life. It makes no sense to concentrate on things that are beyond one's control, given that those things that *are* within one's control are more than a full-time job.

The ability to move on with your life in the face of massive injustice is a critical aspect of getting what you want through rational living. In the words of Voltaire, "Life is thickly sown with thorns, and I know no other remedy than to pass

> It's not a question of whether you will experience injustice, but how you handle it when it makes its appearance.

quickly through them. The longer we dwell on our misfortunes, the greater is their power to harm us."

Thanks to people like John Britten and Jim Blanchard, the way I view injustice has dramatically changed over the years. I now realize that it's not a question of whether or not I will experience injustice, but how I handle it when it makes its appearance—and what I learn from it to apply to other situations—that will decide the course of my life. With this kind of rational perspective, injustices can be transformed into positives that can help a person achieve long-term success.

AFTERWORD: THE ENDGAME

Be happy while you are living,
for you are a long time dead.
SCOTTISH PROVERB

Since the onset of language, happiness has probably been discussed more than any other subject, just a step ahead of love.
Both are difficult to define, but there is one major difference between the two. Love is an emotion; happiness is a state of mind.
Love, we are safe to assume, always produces happiness, but happiness can result from many things other than love. And whatever thing it is that you want in life, the endgame is that it
presumably will make you happy. Achieving happiness, therefore,
is what this book has been about.

If we are to make inroads into achieving happiness, we first
have to understand it. And to do that, we need a starting point,
an axiom, as it were. Anyone can choose to define happiness to
suit himself, but if we use the dictionary as a guide, the words
that are most meaningful to me are "characterized by pleasure,"

pleasure in turn being defined as "a feeling of being pleased." (I would also point out that, just as heat, scientifically speaking, is the absence of cold, pleasure could arguably be defined as the absence of pain.) For purposes of this book, I have therefore used as the definition of happiness "a state of mind characterized by a feeling of pleasure." And getting what you want in life is about as pleasurable as it gets.

What else can lead to happiness other than love? Just about anything. I recall many years ago discussing the subject of money vis-a-vis happiness with an old friend. At one point, I said that I thought it was impossible for a person to be happy if his main focus was on the accumulation of money and material possessions. My friend disagreed, saying that if the accumulation of money and material possessions gave a person pleasure—if it caused him to feel satisfied and gratified—it wasn't up to anyone else to pass judgment on his feelings.

I've never forgotten that insightful comment. Who am I to tell you what makes you happy? Who are you to tell me what makes me happy? Clearly, each of us seeks happiness in our own way. Caring for the poor and sick made Mother Teresa happy; i.e., it gave her pleasure to ease the pain of others. Henry Ford, on the other hand, derived pleasure from mass-producing automobiles. Which of these two did more to make *others* happy is a subject open to debate, but it has nothing to do with the fact that both of these historical figures made decisions that they believed would result in their experiencing the greatest amount of pleasure and least amount of pain. What they had in common was that they were human, and human beings are genetically programmed to gravitate toward pleasure and away from pain. What they did not have in common was a singular method for pursuing happiness.

If we extend this point to its logical conclusion, it is reasonable to assume that a brutal dictator could be happy, a serial killer could be happy, even a criminal-defense attorney could be happy (though he probably would have to remove all mirrors from his home). No matter how offensive we may find the actions of such people to be, their happiness is not about our feelings. It's about *their* feelings. It's about what gives *them* pleasure.

Based on the above, one can see that it's the height of arrogance to try to tell others what should make them happy, yet politicians and self-styled moralists are obsessed with doing just that. Worse, political-action groups take it a step further, achieving their happiness by appealing to the government to use force against those who don't agree with their positions.

Which brings us to the difference between happiness and rational living. Again, a rational life is a life guided by the *conscious effort* to make *rational decisions* that result in an individual's getting what he wants *over the long term*, so long as the actions stemming from those decisions *do not involve the use of force or fraud against anyone else*. Thus, if achieving happiness is the endgame of getting what you want, and rational living is the means to that end, then living a rational life is really about making decisions that result in long-term happiness.

Even so, there are many ways to experience happiness other than by living a rational life. Remember, rational living requires:

1. Conscious effort.

2. Rational decisions.

3. Long-term results.

4. An absence of aggression (i.e., the use of force or fraud).

A person can inherit a million dollars without making a conscious effort to do anything, let alone make rational decisions. He may be very happy with his inheritance, at least for a while. But, remember, living a rational life is not just about happiness; it's about achieving *the greatest amount of happiness over the long term*. Marilyn Monroe was probably happy for a while; Janis Joplin was probably happy for a while; John Belushi was probably happy for a while. Happiness was not the problem for any of these celebrities or for millions of other people who have come to an early dead-end in life. It's *long-term* happiness that was the problem. High-class people make decisions geared to future happiness; low-class people make decisions geared to instant, usually short-lived, happiness.

Thus, a serial killer could experience momentary happiness, though his actions would be appalling to any civilized person. His actions might even be the result of conscious effort, but they would be unlikely to result in long-term happiness. In fact, he probably would experience a great deal of mental pain between murders, in which case his happiness would be very short-lived. In any event, a serial killer would be way out of touch with the doctrine of rational living, simply because he would be achieving his happiness through aggression against others.

A person could, of course, take the position that he doesn't care if he commits aggression against others, so long as he himself is happy. Absolutely true. This book's definition of a rational life is nothing more than my opinion. No one else is obliged to abide by my definition. I personally insist on the non-aggression tag, because I believe that non-aggression is the foundation for natural law; i.e., I believe that every individual has a right to sovereignty over his own life and body, and that no one has a right to violate that sovereignty through the use of force. For me, not committing aggression against others is an important facet of seeking my own long-term happiness. You and you alone must decide how important that condition is to *your* happiness.

The good news is that making decisions geared to long-term happiness does not preclude one from being happy in the short term as well. What it does mean is that a person should not consistently opt for instant gratification without regard to the long-term consequences of his actions. In other words, it's foolish to compartmentalize one's life into the present and future; rather, the two should be viewed as inextricably connected parts of one's life. Thus, to the extent one makes instant-gratification decisions that are in conflict with one's long-term happiness, such decisions will usually prove to be self-destructive.

I'VE ALWAYS FELT that the dumbest question anyone can ask of another person is, "Are you happy?" This is, for obvious reasons, an old favorite of media people who interview celebrities. What makes it so eminently stupid is the fact that there is no such thing as absolute happiness, and, further, no accurate way of quantifying it. Theoretically, you can be happier every day of your life than you were the day before. The gradations are infinite. You can accidentally shoot yourself in the foot, lose your little toe, and be happy that you didn't lose your big toe. Losing your little toe is a painful thing to think about, while not losing your big toe is a pleasant thing to think about.

Our modern-day obsession with happiness has millions of people all over the world chasing their happiness tails. In truth, however, it's a mistake to dwell on happiness. In fact, it's probably not possible to be happy if you're obsessed with achieving happiness. Viktor Frankl referred to this as "paradoxical intention," a phenomenon whereby we decrease our chances of achieving something if we dwell on it too much.

Long-term happiness is a result of making conscious, rational decisions that are in accordance with universal principles—in effect, a result of living a rational life. I think of happiness as the endgame of life, not because it is a state of mind for which you should consciously strive, but because happiness is an end in itself. Happiness is a result—a symptom, as it were—of "living right." So focus on

> Happiness isn't a state of mind for which you should consciously strive, but rather an end result of focusing on the principals that lead to happiness: truth, personal virtue, and the creation of value.

truth, not happiness; focus on creating value, not happiness; focus on personal virtue, not happiness. All of these *lead* to happiness, as sure as day follows night, but focusing on happiness itself is likely to yield only frustration.

If no one else can tell you what makes you happy, then neither can anyone tell you whether or not you *are* happy. Only you know how much pleasure and pain you feel inside. One good way to measure your feelings of pleasure and pain is to take note of how often you find yourself choosing among good alternatives and how often you find yourself choosing among the lesser of two (or more) evils. When you choose between two bad alternatives, you are not choosing to eliminate pain, but only to ease pain as much as possible. When you consciously make rational decisions as to which choices are least painful, it's true that you are following an important guideline for living a rational life. However, if you find yourself choosing among painful alternatives too often, you're probably not doing a very good job of living a rational life.

EXTREME HAPPINESS

When I was in my mid-twenties, I spent a lot of time in New York on business. I didn't have any money to speak of, so I got to know the less trendy parts of Manhattan, Brooklyn, and Queens pretty well. It was an exciting time—high hopes, eternal youth, and a world of opportunity. Sleep was an occasional distraction, gourmet dining was a corned beef sandwich at a Lower East Side deli. I could not have imagined a more exhilarating activity than walking around Greenwich Village, taking the subway to Sheepshead Bay in Brooklyn, or browsing at Macy's on Thirty-fourth Street at a time when only New York could boast of a Macy's store.

I usually stayed at the Prince George Hotel on Twenty-eighth Street, as it was inexpensive and more than suitable for my needs at the time. Best of all, there was an automat just across the street, and when it came to dining treats, the automat was just a notch below my favorite deli. As exciting as those times were for me, I probably did not fully appreciate the magnificence of it all. There was a feeling of urban spirituality that I certainly will never again experience—first, because I will never again be in my mid-twenties; second, because the world was much younger then—much more innocent, much more wholesome.

What I now realize is that I was in a very high state of consciousness, a consciousness that would have been impossible for me to intentionally achieve. In retrospect, I realize that my hyperconscious state was a prerequisite for what was about to happen to me. One beautiful, sunny day in November, I was driving on the Grand Central Parkway on my way to JFK International Airport. My mind was exploding with a thousand and one thoughts about my life, both business and personal. Then, just as I swung past LaGuardia Airport, a remarkable thing occurred.

Instead of having to exert the usual intense mental effort to sort out my thoughts, every item that was of importance to me at that time—perhaps forty or fifty in number—instantly became clearly fixed in my mind in such an orderly fashion that I felt almost omniscient. It seemed as though a bright light had suddenly brought my thoughts out of the dark recesses of my subconscious mind and allowed me to consciously focus on all of them simultaneously.

Though I have not driven to JFK Airport for many years, and, in fact, rarely go to New York anymore, the impact of that event was so great that I still vividly recall steering my car south onto the Van Wyck Expressway as my entire life seemed to freeze into sharp focus. It was as though I were being given the means to solve all my business and personal problems simultaneously. It was an impossible-to-describe feeling of total control.

I do not recall exactly how long that ecstatic feeling of heightened awareness lasted, but I would estimate that it was perhaps two or three minutes in length. Over the years, I have had similar experiences on a handful of occasions, each of them

lasting only a matter of seconds, but nothing to match the intensity of that incredible blink of consciousness I experienced on my way to JFK Airport.

I DID NOT GIVE my remarkable experience with heightened awareness a great deal of thought until some years later when I happened upon a book entitled *Cosmic Consciousness*, by Dr. Richard Maurice Bucke, originally published in 1901. Dr. Bucke was a graduate of McGill Medical School and a prominent psychiatrist in Canada. He died from an accidental fall on the ice, at age sixty-five, a year after his book was published.

At age thirty-six, Dr. Bucke had experienced an "illumination" that lasted only a few seconds, but during which time he claimed to have learned more than he had in years of academic study. Dr. Bucke's metaphysical experience never repeated itself, but he ultimately came to believe that it was the emergence of a new faculty in man that takes simple consciousness to a new level. He hypothesized that such historical figures as Jesus, Buddha, Dante, and even Walt Whitman possessed this advanced consciousness on a consistent basis, while in the rest of us the aptitude is still evolving.

In the last section of *Cosmic Consciousness*, Dr. Bucke documents numerous cases of cosmic consciousness experienced by other individuals whom he interviewed during his lifetime.

SHORTLY AFTER my introduction to the work of Dr. Bucke, one of my readers sent me a letter suggesting I read another book, *Thinking and Destiny*, by Harold W. Percival. This thousand-page work is, to say the least, not the easiest of reading, but the author's foreword alone is worth the price of the book:

> From November of 1892 I passed through astonishing and crucial experiences, following which, in the spring of 1893,

there occurred the most extraordinary event of my life. I had crossed 14th Street at 4th Avenue, in New York City. Cars and people were hurrying by. While stepping up to the northeast corner curbstone, Light, greater than that of myriads of suns opened in the center of my head. In that instant or point, eternities were apprehended. There was no time. Distance and dimensions were not in evidence. . . . I was conscious of Consciousness as the Ultimate and Absolute Reality. . . . It would be futile to attempt description of the sublime grandeur and power and order and relation in poise of what I was then conscious. Twice during the next fourteen years, for a long time on each occasion, I was conscious of Consciouness. But during that time I was conscious of no more than I had been conscious of in that first moment.

IN A RELATED INCIDENT, some years later I heard the following story from a perfect stranger ("Dan") during a chance encounter while taking a stroll by the ocean. As our conversation unfolded, Dan explained that he had been searching for a long time for a feeling he had experienced many years before. He had been a successful young stock broker, until, one day, he realized he wasn't happy and quit his job.

He then went on to tell me that he bought a quaint little house in a modest neighborhood, packed away his business suits, and bought several pairs of overalls. At first, he spent most of his time fixing up the house and relaxing. Then, after a while, he started making stained-glass windows in his garage and selling them to people in the neighborhood. He vividly recalled how happy he was in his new life.

What he remembered most of all was a specific point in time when he was sitting on the front steps of his house. He said that his mind was completely relaxed, and that it was the only time in his life that he could remember that happening to him. Then, without warning, he experienced a feeling of contentment throughout his body, a sensation he referred to as "total joy." He said he was conscious of wanting to freeze that moment in time for eternity.

Dan concluded his tale by saying, "For fifteen years I've been searching, hoping to recapture that feeling of ecstasy . . . searching for it . . . believing it's out there somewhere . . . but no matter how hard I try, it always seems beyond my reach."

NONE OF THE EXPERIENCES I have just described were identical in nature. Nevertheless, all of them possess at least two common threads. First, there was the sudden onset of each phenomenon; second, there was some kind of heightened state of awareness. Call it metaphysics, call it spirituality, call it enlightenment, but the evidence suggests that what was afoot here was something far beyond our normal secular existence, something that elevates one's awareness to a level at which he becomes "conscious of consciousness."

For the duration of this chapter, I have arbitrarily chosen to refer to this advanced mental state as *joy*. By dictionary definition, joy is "an emotion of great happiness." I would be tempted to refer to it as ultimate happiness, but that would raise the same question I have with absolute happiness; i.e., there is no accurate way to quantify either happiness or joy. The truth is that none of us can ever be certain about what constitutes ultimate happiness.

It would therefore seem logical to assume that joy—extreme happiness identifiable by a higher-than-secular awareness—can vary in intensity. At one end of the joy spectrum would be Percival's experience of being conscious of consciousness and Bucke's momentary connection to the cosmos. At the other end of the spectrum could be just about any experience you may have had that clearly stands out above other happy moments in your life. It could be a spring afternoon when you were a teenager, walking home with your sweetheart . . . or sitting among 80,000 screaming fans at an important college football game, feeling the chill of snow flurries blowing against your face . . . or walking on the beach at sunrise with a surreal sense of connection to every atom in the universe.

Whatever it is, joy seems to invite itself into our lives without warning. I vividly recall my seventeenth birthday on a beautiful and sunny winter Saturday. I hung out most of the day with my pals, fully focused on reaching unprecedented heights of teenage coolness. Other than Eskimos, it would have been impossible for anyone to have been as cool as we thought we were on that glorious day. There was a distinct flair to the way we loosely held our cigarettes between our thumb and forefinger that would have made James Dean proud. We cruised all the important spots in town. We had burgers and fries at the Town House Drive-In. We generously stopped by a few of the sharper gals' homes to offer our best, nonsensical high-school chatter, the sole purpose of which was to reinforce our coolness. On that particular winter day, Payton Place belonged to us. For at least a brief period of time, we were, to borrow a phrase from Tom Wolfe's *The Bonfire of the Vanities,* masters of the universe.

I was in a groove, one that I had never before experienced, and one that I was far too young to understand. I was certain of only two things. First, that I was immortal; second, that everything I touched would instantly turn to gold. It was only fitting that I had a basketball game to play that evening. While shooting outside shots during warm-ups, I felt as if a large tube had been inserted between my hand and the basket, and that all I needed to do was throw the ball through the tube. I scored forty-two points that night—at a time when there was no such thing as a three-point shot! I don't recall the ball ever leaving my hand without my being certain that it was going to touch nothing but net. It was almost scary.

After the game, my pals and I attended a dance, and there I met a beautiful young girl whom just about every guy in the school coveted. As high schoolers are adept at doing, she let it be known to others that she had a crush on me. That led to slow, romantic dancing, an evening of getting to know each other, and a finish that probably would have today's high school inmates totally perplexed and snickering.

The joyful day I have just described preceded my New York experience by some eight years. I decided to share it with you as a way of making the point that joy comes in many shapes and sizes. You've probably had at least one day similar to the one I just described when everything just seemed to be perfect. Most likely you can recall the day, and possibly even joy's moment of onset, very clearly, as well as the circumstances surrounding it.

Is there a connection between my cool at age seventeen and an experience as dramatic as the Light in the center of Harold Percival's head? I cannot say with certainty, but my suspicion is that they are, indeed, related. While I would not presume to speak on behalf of any of the people whose stories I have shared with you, I have inferred that in each case there was a feeling of joy, i.e., extreme happiness.

The corollary to this might be that simple happiness is but a diluted form of joy. When we experience moments or entire days like the day of my seventeenth birthday, I think what we are experiencing is what I would call "elementary joy." Our human senses have the capacity to elevate a secular event beyond the level of its true importance, such as what Mark McGwire must have been feeling—indeed, what all those watching were feeling—when he smashed his sixty-second home run to break Roger Maris's thirty-seven-year-old record. This kind of elation, I believe, is joy in its most elementary form.

If true joy is, in fact, just an extreme form of happiness, why does it visit us so rarely and so unexpectedly? Because there is no anticipation of joy; joy is the present. You can't plan to be joyful any more than you can plan to be happy. Keeping in mind the dangers of paradoxical intention, one must always be wary not to focus on joy itself, but, rather, on those principles that lead to joy. I believe that you go about pursuing joy the same way you go about pursuing happiness, which is to say that you don't consciously pursue it at all. As many people reach their golden years, particularly people of means, they often find themselves asking the age-old question, "Is that all there is?" The probable catalyst in such cases is that there is too much focus on happiness itself, rather than on those things that lead to happiness.

If, as I have suggested, living a rational life results in long-term happiness, then one could speculate that experiencing joy is the ultimate result of rational living. It is likely that we invite joy into our lives through a pure mind, a mind cleansed of secular poison ranging from envy to stress to idle chatter to focusing on meaningless activities. I believe that joy, on those rare occasions when it visits us, is the result of making conscious, rational decisions that are in accordance with universal principles, which, above all, includes a relentless search for, and discovery of, truth. Leonardo da Vinci hinted at this when he observed that "the noblest pleasure is the joy of understanding," which I find to be a most interesting combination of words— *pleasure, joy,* and *understanding* all in one short sentence. Understanding is a result of a successful search for truth, which da Vinci referred to as joyful, and joy is extreme pleasure.

> Experiencing joy is the ultimate result of rational living.

So how does one achieve a permanent state of joy, i.e., extreme happiness? I think it's safe to say that such an ongoing state of mind is not possible on a secular plane. In fact, happiness on any level cannot be ongoing, because pain is an integral and important part of life. Pain gives us a reference point for experiencing pleasure. Ill health gives us a reference point for experiencing the pleasure of good health; poverty gives us a reference point for experiencing the pleasure of wealth; losing gives us a reference point for experiencing the pleasure of winning. Life itself would not be precious to us without the reality of death.

Therefore, while the objective of living a rational life is to make decisions that result in more pleasure and less pain, it is critically important to accept pain as a normal part of life. Think of pain as a teacher. Learn from it. Use it for personal growth. Ironically, to reduce the amount of pain in your life, it is important not to fight pain. To fight pain sets in motion a sort of reverse paradoxical intention, i.e., the more you focus on not experiencing pain, the less likely you are to eliminate it.

Finally, as you make your way through life with a heightened awareness of the importance of making rational decisions that result in more long-term pleasure and less pain, never lose sight of the fact that there are many people in this world who do not want others to be happy. There are people who seemingly work full-time at trying to convince you that it is your moral obligation to submit to their wills. Their objective is to cajole and intimidate you into subordinating your interests, goals, and happiness to theirs.

You are unlikely to convince such people that their actions are, at best, misguided; at worst, immoral. That being the case, let them live their lives as they so choose. The consequences of their actions will be *their* consequences, not yours. If, by contrast, you choose to focus on achieving your long-term goals by living a rational life, your actions will harm no one. To the extent you are successful, you will be in a position to make constructive contributions to loved ones, and, through the wonders of the marketplace, to the world in general.